Also by W.B.

Fiction:

Ring Around the Rosy

Astoria Strange

The Files of Milky Dent

Poetry:

Minor Revelations

Dictation from the Backyard

There Were Elms

The Automatic Poems

Non-Fiction:

Get in the Car

Zine:

I Remember My Life

Weather

Nine Months of a Weekday Milieu

W.B. Cushman

These are Monday through Friday Blog posts,
lifted with permission from couchsurfingat70

ISBN: 9798756728422

Editor: W.B. Cushman

Cover photo: W.B. Cushman

Cover design: W.B. Cushman

Formatting: Sarco Press

For my friends through the ages

Contents

Introduction

The titles of each daily post from the Blog which follow are set in 14-point type. Everything else is the predictable 12. All in "Times New Roman" font. (Well, every once in a while I slip in "Lucinda Handwriting – I like its look.) Everything is justified to the left. There are two space returns between the end of one post and the title of the next. The three sections of the book, while factually reporting when those posts begin, were carved out arbitrarily, pretty much to allow the reader to give it a moment and take a breath. Like a rest stop on Interstate 5.

This Introduction is primarily math. The first post in "January", from the 22nd of that month, explains things clearly enough. No reason to repeat myself. I will say these posts appear nearly exactly as they were viewed in that weekday's Blog. Alternate spellings, funky arrangements of sentences, playful connections of nouns and verbs. Just the way readers saw them then. Where 'Word' has applied a blue underline, the program figuring there's a punctuation change to make the reading more readable, I have made many of those changes. Why not. The goal, always, is make the reading as easy and interesting and engaging as possible. I don't want a missing comma to mess with that. Likewise, I've removed one of my million "ands" here and there, and begun new sentences.

Otherwise, what you have here is what the Blog offered – free – to subscribers every Monday through Friday between the 22nds of January and October – 2021.

I don't think there's anything else to say.

January

Weather – January 22, 2021

Posts here at 'Couch Surfing at 70' have been few and far between the last number of months, a psychic break from the one-after-another 2020 '30:30' timed-writing blurbs which morphed into the bulk of "The Files of Milky Dent", that book ultimately taking most of my writing energy within the process of editing and revising. Excuses and facts, the truth, and, yeah, not a lot happening here on the Blog.

Which is about to change.

Later last night, up in the blue recliner, a thought came to me - this ('Couch Surfing') is my space, paid for and owned, and there is an opportunity to better use it. The arriving idea being to come up with what I'll call a "daily weather report", weather in this case being thoughts, feelings, considerations, 'aha' bursts, cool and fun ideas, wacky weirdness, an endless parade of mental imagery which - me being a writer - I then come running down here to the keyboard and spill out into this waiting Blog space - like, rave on, Brah.

Specifically, my plan going forward is showing up here every day, Mondays through Fridays, and letting spill out of the old noggin', heart, and soul whatever's going on with and for me that day, what I'm thinking about, what I'm feeling, ideas and issues crowding in amidst the me of me. And being a writer and being a blogger and believing a primary purpose, a calling, for me on the planet is to write stuff and share it with the hope that the planet is better off for it. Of course, with the clarity that what the reader - You - does with it is his/her/your business, which includes shining it on and going about with something you like better. For me, it's like my old high school friend Donnie always said -- all I can do is all I can do.

So - here goes. I have in mind something like a journal entry, even a post-it note to myself to think about later, somedays as long as 1500 words, others a single sentence. I won't know until I get there. And I'm not **there**, a future there, today. I'm **here**, this Friday, January 22, 2021, three days after my unique clock rang up 72 years visiting the planet. I'll have (and post) what I'm thinking about **today** in a while, maybe an hour, maybe five or six. If I'm lucky enough to still be here next Monday, remembering what Charles on Boston's WBCN radio said daily back in the 60's/70's – "If the creek don't rise and there ain't no meltdown" - I'll Blog what strikes me as worth recording Monday. It might be anything.

Daily weather reports. The me of me. Starting today.

Twists in the Road

This morning, sitting in the mauve, living-room recliner, sipping hot coffee, I found myself slipping back through the time and times of my life - these 72 years - and it came to me I had experienced four moments through all that time where causes and conditions, a specific event or two leading the way, had had a profound impact on my life. Such that, following, I would never be the same again. Four moments.

Sometime in the fall of 1968 into the spring of 1969 my view of life, and include here culture, society, and politics, underwent a metamorphosis from leaning Republican to lifelong (secret handshake) membership in the American

Yippie party. A kid from my high school was killed in Vietnam. I went to his funeral and could make absolutely no sense of it. Just before this, or just after, I attended a lecture at Cape Cod Community College, where I was a student, by William J. Lederer, author of a book titled "The Ugly American", and in the lecture he described a recent journey through Vietnam and the things he'd seen - lies and duplicity and downright evil perpetrated by the US government on the people of Vietnam, and as significantly, on its (our) own people. At that time there was a group on campus, the 'Union for Student Involvement', a bunch of long hairs and hippies and guys and gals who we'd label radicals nowadays, and all of a sudden what they were saying - what they'd been saying - made perfect sense to me.

In the fall of 1968 I'd held a Richard Nixon sign at the Hyannis rotary. By the fall of '69, having started up a USI chapter at my new school up in Salem, I was sitting in and picketing, writing leftist screeds, and generally checking out from the mainstream of life. Forever.

That's Number One.

The late winter of 1983 I was crashing on my little sister's couch in Somerville, MA, just back from yet another gonna-live-there-forever excursion out to California (bus rides back and forth). I owned two trash bags of personal items which were stashed in a friend's cellar in Medford. I'd managed to buy a weird used car ('69 Sunbeam) and land a job as a youth outreach worker for a brand-new kid Drug and Alcohol Counseling/Outreach/Referral program in Stoneham. I was there, at work, the afternoon of April 15, 1983, which was a Friday, sitting in on a training by a guy talking with the few of us staff about working with junior high kids around smoking pot, risks, and stuff. But that's not what I heard. What I heard was this guy talking to me, and just to me, all about me. I could have been alone in a cave with this dude, him a reformed junkie at a methadone clinic in Allston. The afternoon went away, I lost track of time after work, something about driving up and down Route 1 hour after hour. When I got back to my sister's place just after 11:30 there were four 16-ounce cans of my Ballantine Ale in her refrigerator. I stood in her kitchen and drank two of them. April 15th, 1983.

The next day was my Saturday to cover the program and I showed up but ducked out at noon. I drove up to Stoneham High School and began running on the school's track. I was there by myself. It's funny what I remember, with all I don't, but I ran that circle 28 times that Saturday, seven miles, and on the 14th time around (keeping count on my fingers) I heard someone say, "I'm an alcoholic." I was the only one there. When I finished running, I drove back to my sister's, opened the fridge, grabbed the two remaining cans of Ballantine and poured them down my sister's sink.

I have not had one drink or one drug since. Number Two.

In the summer of 2008 I was sleeping in a spare room with friends in Harwich, again on Cape Cod, running the housing program for the Aids Support Group in Provincetown and - as has been my way - hankering for something else. I began driving after work to the Chocolate Sparrow Coffee Shop in Orleans and writing cover letters for jobs all over the country, mostly kid jobs. I must have sent out 50 resumes and received not one offer. But, along the way I found myself sending lots to Portland, Oregon, and having never set foot in the Northwest and knowing not one soul, with no job waiting, of course it made good sense to me to move there. So, I left my worldly goods in a storage unit and drove to Vancouver, Washington, where I'd rented a room on Craigslist. This was September '08. Four months later I moved to Portland and found a kid job, and on September 24th, 2009, I went on what we used to call "blind dates" with a woman I'd met on Match.Com. The following September 24th we got married in Virginia, combining wedding and honeymoon.

Ah, Susan. Changed my life. Gave me the space to grow in all kinds of cool and unexpected ways. Magical, mystical partner.

Meeting Susan was Number Three.

I left our house (Susan's, I rent) on a hot-as-a-mother day in July or August in 2018, and went for a walk "down low" along the Johnson Creek. I was most of the way home before I made or received (the memory thing again) a phone call from my best pal Gavin in Oakland, CA. During the conversation he began telling me about a diet called Keto, how they'd used it to treat mentally challenged kids back in the 50's, he was doing it, some of the specifics of what you could and couldn't and really wanted to eat. His big excitement. By the time I'd got home I'd decided to give it a try, like, why not? So, I told Susan and she said she'd like to try it too and about that time I was up to a weight of 181 and 15 minutes ago I weighed myself and the digital numbers read 149.4, and I have to tell you the weight thing, while real nice and comforting in many ways, isn't the best of it. Blood numbers (better ones) and brain-cell fireworks. Tangibles and intangibles, all trending wicked better.

Keto - was Number Four.

So, this is what I was thinking about hours ago, this is what came to me this morning, this is my weather report for the day, like I posted earlier I was going to share, begin sharing one every weekday moving on. This one longer than most will be, no doubt, really fun to drift back and remember stuff. Details, children. It be in the details.

Or you might say - Shake it up Baby. Twist and Shout.

Any Given Day

I was running a tad slow earlier this morning, before the light of day, before the call of chickens down the street, before even the mile-away peacocks. Sort of casual, I was, and digging it, all the ambiance and evidence of abundance and ways to find small joys, delight, within my own creations and expanding creativity. Which these days I think of as doing my part to save the planet.

We, my wife Susan and I, streamed the movie "Soul" last night, Sunday night at the movies at the Cushman's. "Soul" was quite wonderful, a message to follow our bliss, which maybe takes a while to figure out - our bliss - just what the unique drive to be more 'this' human is, be more involved.......more giving. On the path along the way to the big "Aha". Ah - so this is it. Living and appreciating life, giving, and maybe whisked right back to "Now I lay me down to sleep." Remember? To hopefully acknowledge any good done. Any at all. Dues for this life.

A blessing of life, the fact I am flat out amazed when I get another day, and as such, when on my morning knees asking for a grateful heart, I do not forget to say thanks. Thanks a lot. I'm still here.

I say this alone, quietly, in the earliness, the still-dark, I say please help me to have a grateful heart today, and thanks a lot that I'm still here. I ask for help to be myself as a storyteller as well, to be the me of me, writer, doodler. Yours truly.

Perhaps this morning, now some hours ago and fading, I thought about last night's movie, a Sunday at the Cushman's with a sweet dose of soul, and thought what my long-ago friend and mentor Dick M was forever saying to me - "You're right where you're supposed to be."

The Pieces I Am, Too

This morning early, up there in the living-room recliner, I finished reading Toni Morrison's "The Bluest Eye", the paperback with her 1993 Afterword. My first thought, closing the book, was to run down here to the basement and gather every unsold copy of the books I have written and not sold and set fire to them all. Then open this very 'Couch Surfing' Blog site and delete every word I've ever posted. Never in a million years, I knew closing that "Bluest" back cover, would I, could I write with the majesty and grace and power that Toni did. Fortunately those impulses passed, an "I Am the Walrus" I am me and you are you and we are all together thing, yes, like that. It all goes into the wash, Bro, and we writers create, we do the best we can with the words we're provided at any given time and we add to the wondrous world of language. Vive la difference, and it's good to have goals. So, I had another cup of coffee instead.

How I came to be finishing a Toni Morrison book on this Tuesday morning pretty much followed a Hansel and Gretel-like path. Three days into 2021 I was suddenly compelled to come up with New Year's resolutions, something I'd not done for a gazillion years, and I wrote down three. One was to watch/stream a video documentary every week for the next year, offer stimulating, informational, worthy material to the then 71-year old brain cells. Toward the honorary Doctoral degree I'll be awarding myself one of these decades. I shared my resolve with my wife Susan and she dug it and a week later we brought dinner out before the television and watched Hulu's "Toni Morrison: The Pieces I Am." It was wonderful and deeply moving, dramatically inspiring, and I knew immediately I'd been so lucky to see it. Coincidentally, my birthday (72nd) was coming up in a couple of weeks and having been unable to previously offer an answer to the "What do you want?" question, I now said how about "The Bluest Eye". Yeah - I got it. "Beloved" too.

I also received for my birthday "Always Outnumbered, Always Outgunned" by Walter Mosley, an author whose writing I have long cherished, which I finished four days ago. Currently, remaining directly before the recliner on the coffee table, waiting for its turn, is "The Leroi Jones/Amiri Baraka Reader". I bought that for myself on Ebay. Cheap. Couple months back.

All three of these named writers are African-American. Only Mosley still lives this Tuesday morning. Their color is a fact, do with it what you will. What happened for me, in the recliner, after I let go my urge to "451" my books, was the thought of how lucky I was to grow up in the town of Wareham, Massachusetts. To grow up in the company of black kids, friends, and black families, and a milieu - not always - but almost always of harmony and, following the harmony, a resulting richness of life. My life.

Lucky to watch the Toni Morrison documentary. Lucky to grow up in Wareham. Lucky one of those black Wareham high school kids and me were roommates sophomore year at Cape Cod Community. Another person inspiring my life. Lucky, lucky, lucky.

This is me Tuesday. This is my Tuesday early. My weather report, the where I am at. Today.

Times

I entered the Fred Meyer grocery store just after 8:15 this morning, holding a shopping list of weekly foods for my son Spenser - who was home asleep in a warm bed. In addition to the shopping list, I had in my long, hand-me-down coat left pocket a rag soaked in bleach, zipped in a plastic bag, and a bottle of Trader Joe hand sanitizer in my right coat pocket. My phone, left front jeans pocket, was off, not to be touched out in the populated social world, and the plastic debit card in the right front pocket, already free from the wallet.

I was wearing a face mask.

I took the bleached rag and thoroughly washed down the handles of a small shopping cart, and in the store did my best to stay away from shoppers (not a lot) and employees (tons), the store undergoing a big remodel. When I paid at a solo check-out I pushed the card into the reader, and having to tap in the four-digit pin, took the bottle of hand sanitizer and cleansed my hands before leaving - again before directing the key fob to pop open the trunk - and once more before turning the ignition and touching all kinds of driving stuff in the car.

When I arrived home and was let in an open door, I washed my hands a long time in soap and hot water, bleached lightly everything I'd bought with the same rag, everything not going in the freezer, save for the avocados (for Susan and me) and potatoes (Spenser and Marie). I bleached the kitchen counter, the fridge and freezer handles and inside refrigerator shelvings I'd touched, kitchen cabinets I'd opened, and every doorknob in and out of the kitchen and house front and back doors. For kicks I bleached the mailbox. Then I washed my hands with soap and hot water again.

I'm 72. I've had the first of the two vaccination shots. This routine just described is played out with every weekly trip to Fred Meyer's, every other week to Trader Joe's. Other than walks, I don't go anywhere else.

Are these the times that try men's (and women's) souls? I suppose we each get to say. Somewhat, of course, for sure. For me, I was darn happy I got to wake up again today. Pretty fucking glad.

Friday way Approximations

5 a.m. Meditation

7 a.m. Morning Pages

9 a.m. - Zoom meeting

10 a.m. - Finished one book, began another

11 a.m. - Long walk through the Hood

Noon - Mailed "Milky Dent" and Greeting Card to San Fran

1 p.m. - Coffee and heavy reading

2 p.m. - Electric trim beard, hair....shower

3 p.m. - Thank you note/free card to (8) Patrons

4 p.m. - Friday weigh-in with Spenser (me, 148.2 lbs)

Friday night with wife Susan - To be continued.......

Banger oh Banger

Banger oh Banger. This is me (this me), I'm sure Walt Whitman approves, my exuberant self, especially with these vows of silence and heavy noticing.

My pal Milky Dent has a belief and always believes it's about compassion, which he and his posse of energy minstrels chase hourly. It's the compassion, Brah (they always say).

And you won't find me - Banger - disagreeing ever, no doubt Walt Whitman ain't either, him getting to sleep and getting to wake up and getting to look around and see stuff. Celebrating that.

Oh Banger my Banger.

Giving Normal the Finger

Well here we go Thursday, my mind electric and I'm thinking evermore in the place and space of 'just this'.

"This." My complete sentence.

Yeah, I'm reading another book about Zen, an occasionally

interesting memoir, but the spectacular nuggets, didn't the early forty-niners note just a tiny gleam of gold under flowing waters - and that was enough. Always enough. Oh, to be a panhandler.

My, the vision of panhandling, so interesting, especially now here on Thursday morning and not only some street corner or from an apartment building doorway. Golden slumber panhandles everywhere.

Anyway, pretty sure I'm down to "Just This" now more than most the rest of my 72 plus years, dig it, so far anyhows, which I've been allowed on this planet.

'This' feels right.

Peanut's Poem

I stand tall within myself -

Outside too.

Viewable but effervescent.

Isn't there always a peanut gallery

Or two

Worth Ignoring?

Scrambled Kiss

Tuesday:

Antwon Alazar is sitting alone in his barber shop. The sign out front says "Antwon's Hair Cutting". Old school.

Antwon is a white dude, just so you know in case you were surmising otherwise. Which explains the fact of his favorite meal being scrambled eggs. Antwon's a "keep it simple" guy and creating a meal of scrambled eggs is darned simple. It begins with gathering ingredients – dab of bacon fat, eggs. That's it. Sometimes when he wants to get way crazy, like one of those gone cats Kerouac said were "mad for life", he'll grate in shavings of pepper-jack cheese – Oh, you go go wild man, way out there on the freakin' edge Brah. Dig it. Love it. Bacon fat dab, eggs, bitchin' cheese. In fact, from here out I'm never using the term "keep it simple" or the preferred "keep it simple stupid" ever again. No need, Snead. Ima gonna write the words 'scrambled eggs' and that'll be metaphor enough.

Simple is Antwon's thing, and for your information the whole nom de plume deal was his parents – Freddie and Gina Alazar, former Yippies and edge creatures themselves -- they figured you name a honkey baby Antwon it won't take but by the second grade when a host of white supremacists come into little Antwon's life (yes, still in big Antwon's too) and get right up in his grill, them offended by a white guy with what you expect to be an Afro-American's name, meaning, Freddie and Gina figured, little to big Antwon would go through life with a never-ending supply of opportunities to have to deal with racist, stupid motherfuckers, which of course was/ is the real deal and early on Antwon – a true devotee of the movie and even monaural album "West Side Story" -- began carrying a zip gun, a 50's thing and a favorite among kids of all colors and religious propensities from poorer neighborhoods, so little (second grade) Antwon scored one from a very cool uncle (Gina's crazy ass brother Howler) and began zipping that baby on shitheads everywhere, by third grade with a reputation nearly as wild as adding pepper-jack to your scrambles, and just like Brian Wilson and Mike Love would be predicting a few years down the road, "The bad guys know us and they leave us alone", which is how it went down.

And moving out from home when he quit school sophomore year to do a stint in VISTA and then a couple of moves around to different cities, yeah, you got to get that rep built up all over again and again, and he would and did and Gina and Freddie pat themselves on the back to this day doing right by their boy, and 19 months ago Antwon was offered a free ride at the Livinia Levesque Hair Styling academy and followed his mantra of strange travel suggestions carry you out to the edge and (remember that crazy mofo Uncle Howler) a relative hit the lottery and staked him to a year's rent of a sitting-empty barber shop down off 14th Street in Oakland, a couple blocks up from the city library and, aside from all-alone meditations like when we entered this tale, Antwon makes enough to bring home the bacon (Ha!! Yes!! You maniac. Eggs, cheese and freakin' bacon!!)

Which I hope you'll agree is a fine old happy ending.

Velvets

It is said the Buddha's final words were, "Be a lamp unto this world."

Which is, conceivably, alike the spiritual suggestion, "This little light of mine, I'm gonna let it shine."

Who knows. Myself, I lean toward the Velvet Underground's, "I'll be your mirror, reflect who you are."

And did you know I share a birthday with Janis Joplin. She was once quoted as saying, "It's all the same fucking day, man."

Possibly you had to be there.

Chimes of freedom flashing....

Tell me where the chimes sound

I personally cannot wait to get to the ocean again. Portland sucks. One hundred miles away. I cannot wait for the fresh, cool snappy ocean air, right there, right there, fill my lungs with that oh so much wonder.

How much wonder do we note, accrue in our minds and who knows your answer, yours sort of a whatever for me unless you're a fave of mine, so few these days, man, two of my best ever, main vein connected friends gone so long, Bob, Doug, electric memory, I can tell you they dug the wonder, freakin' count on that.

Yeah - the chimes of freedom flashing, that's what Dylan wrote, and thank goodness for Dylan and thank goodness for chimes and the places they sweetly sound, for me like the ocean air and bare feet in meadows, North Beach, the feel of sneakers on the flat solid sand, breakers just there, folding over from Japan I bet, scoot wave scoot, and I've got The Airplane volumed in the background and me filling up with visions down here in the cellar and Ferlinghetti's gone and most all those with-it cats and the planet's generally a shit show and political parties blow, and even if I have a feel for the answer I think it's worth asking, surely on a Friday.......

Tell me where the chimes sound...

Permissions for Joy

Rat traps, rat traps - I don't believe there will ever be enough rat traps. So the mind tumbles down the basement stairs, no surprises, no promises, just another day, which should go without saying "Thank you God" though otherwise no promise that any of it will get any better. Not all better - even simply plain old better. No promise of that.

Not with Lawrence Ferlinghetti dead, gone away for good and I swear when I saw it, some internet buzz line, I felt the planet shift. Honest, I swear I did. And when I woke the following morning, a middle-of-the-week Wednesday, I felt I'd been given new permissions. Sure of it, clear as if I was back in Oahu on a North Shore beach, super-hot and tropical and wonderful - that degree of clarity, and possibly (there in Hawaii) I may have run into Charles Laquidara on that beach which would have been nice, him another volunteer for gentle planetary kindness, but I didn't though those days with the wife were the best.

I awoke with that degree of clarity that the planet had shifted for the worse, with Ferlinghetti gone, and with new permissions to do my own thing. Yeah, I woke up like that.

And like they said back at the Wareham Park Department storage/hideout shed - "Fuck the raingear."

Angels

(Last week's weather.)

On the third day without electric, without heat, Wednesday, with all those taken-for-granted slices-of-life missing, my wife's handyman called, early in the morning, and asked if we needed firewood. In fact, my wife had decided the night before – the house growing colder each day – to light an early fire and keep it burning through all our waking hours. I'd suggested driving about looking for firewood for sale, charging one cell phone or another within the driving, and we'd decided on that and now here comes this early call out of nowhere other than being blessed and cared for and an hour later this dude – his name is Christian – shows up with two large plastic barrels, one with cut pieces of lumber and large round hunks of wood, the other with small kindling pieces, he drags to the porch and we all masked discuss the lack of power and the gift of fire and the larger gift of kindness and thoughtfulness and he says there are compressed sawdust and other natural burnable ingredient logs for sale up at Mt, Scott, a few miles away, and they throw off glorious heat and he will go and pick up a big bunch for us, and the wife gives him a twenty and a one and half an hour later he is back with 21 logs and tarps to cover from porch rain, milk crates in which to fill and store,

And we burn one after another along with traditional firewood all day, until close to nine that night – Wednesday – and there is a sense of warmth within a 10-foot range, it's a blessing, and the family huddles there often and when the ashes fade to quiet we crawl under the seven blankets and comforters on the bed and our 98-degree bodies fuel that space and just at midnight I am woken by my wife's shout – "A light" – and we rejoice in the return of electricity and don't forget how we have been cared for even here in these days of cold and darkness and missing.

Today.......Verse

(Last week's weather.)

A Poem

The wife sometimes frets, suffers, fleeing from joy. I take Coleman-stove coffee, surely of the wife's skill, none of mine, to the reading recliner, ancient appearance, bought well-used upon entry to these Northwests (now lit here only by day) -

I feel wild with joy, oh, dear sweet coffee and - think of it - not a racist in sight, giddy with awareness of blessings, all the while filled with magical thinking, here it comes, here comes the electricity. But not to be.

I'll fill my non-electric life with charcoal drawings, daylight stories, and coffees the wife's willing ways work (where the do do sends the don't don't on its shruggy out-a-here).

Hangout with my streaming-scuttled kid, is there juice in the laptop for Disney? A stroll then through these slushed streets, will they sound a city horn, I wonder, announce an electric return?

Will I take less for granted tomorrow, even later today, my Tuesday, in this wilderness of darker, colder, now....... though the wife and me do note among each other this norm of the homeless, why we make donations in hopes they help. Some.

For me, the rare carbohydrate left in this past-70 body shoo'd off by celebrating bloodstream Coleman caffeine, oh, thank you blessed wife - though there's something wrong with my left foot (months now) even before the lights went out,

I'll give my books, stack after stack, another hug, it's my way, and we'll own these daylight hours blessed.

Sure to compliment the coffee chef - keeping hope alive.

Shine in the Dark

(Last week's weather.)

During the recent power outage we piled seven blankets and comforters on the bed. I crawled under that warming weight at 6:36 the first night, so very early against the cold, but my wife came and rescued me from my hiding. I returned to the living and made charcoal drawings by battery-lamp light.

First Thing

Nearly the first thing I do every morning is look at the rat traps. I like it when they're empty. Who wants to see death first off? Not me.

Then that's over and the rest of the day proceeds. On its own sweet time, and that 'time' thing is a bit nebulous since of course the second-hand on the wall clock jumps ahead right on schedule, always, as sure as math, but the concept of time remains more personal. Like it can be an individual thing, so a brother and sister sip after-dinner coffee and he says, “Boy, this day really flew by” and she says, “It dragged on forever to me” and neither is right or wrong and on the wall the clock’s second-hand is an impassive observer, so when, (with me) after scanning the rat traps I say, “Then that’s over and the rest of the day proceeds”, how that reads (feels) is up to you.

Which is all I’ve got, early. And my loved doodle.

Just Desert

(A vision)

I pictured myself, earlier, wandering through a desert scene, Nevada likely, a quarter mile off the 15, talking out loud to no one there, trying, really trying, to have a dialogue with some God. Pretty much any God would do. Something wise and just, ancient, or maybe freshly brand new today, mother father kindly neighbor. The grandmother I never had. Most of my out-loud pleading confined to “Please help us”. Please, please help us.

It’s not so hot out there, today, the desert air is fresh, clean, stimulating, long-ago rises of mountains and plateaus stretch the horizon, I wonder do they actually move because I’ve got to figure they do, even if it’s waiting until 3 am when the only possible witness would be a drunk and the sadness in his or her heart tends to blot out beauty. You know? Yes, there are buzzards circling now but they don’t mind me, there’s always another way to make a living. I haven’t seen a snake and sometimes I do look down but more I look at the big landscape, ‘cause there has to be a God or two out here, I mean, ‘come on, would you look at that’.

What happens (in my vision), after a couple of hours, is I decide to write my message in the sand, I kind of dig my sneaker in and drag it along, you know the way kids and sometimes adults make marks, tell stories in the sand or on the dirt, like a treasure map or a plan or something, so I spend maybe 25 minutes dragging my foot through the warmed-up earth, it's tannish, it's sandy with mixes of I don't know materials, and I spell out "please help", all small letters and after I walk back to the Camry pulled off the shoulder of the interstate and there happens to be no cars whizzing by, toward LA, toward Vegas, and I sit there - driver's seat, door open - and think I could have been doing a lot of things not so worthy, not like this owning my own in a good, healthy, affirming, joyful way, and I'll turn the key in the ignition and pull a u-ee and head off west.

Chasing the day.

Keep the Faith

In the 60's and in the 70's you'd often hear someone say to someone else, or hear someone say to you, or hear yourself saying to someone this:

Keep the Faith.

Keep

the

Faith.

They are an interesting trio of words. Suggestion? Command? Prayer? Encouragement? Blessing? Hope? Soul connection? Some? All? I can hear those three words as I sit here now, this Tuesday, and I hear them, perhaps their echoes, as a joined supporting, a we're in this together, a we'll get through this, an I got you, you can do it, you'll be okay.

I like 60's "stuff", that eternal cosmic ambiance somewhere back there on the calendar and alive most days within me. I remain aware of the message. Keep the Faith, Baby. Some days it's like lacing up roller skates and just gliding along with it. Oh yeah, I'm keeping the faith, Sister. I'm good, Brother. Some days it's harder. Today a bit. Me, a citizen of these United States. A crazy kid, dragging along all kinds of aches and pains with the hope for a better day. Or, at least another one just as good.

I'll go with soul connection.

Keep the faith.

Don't Cost Nothing

I drove my wife Susan and I to the Portland Airport last night where we received our second Moderna vaccine injections. The deal, they say, is it'll take another four weeks for the vaccine to kick into its highest gear and provide me (us) with the promise of 95% protection from becoming sick with the Covid virus. Beyond that, medical folks say, if I happen to be one of the unlucky five-percent who still manages to become infected, the chances that it will kill me drop to zero, and in fact any symptoms I have will be significantly diminished from never receiving the vaccine. Which is pretty cool, what with me 72-plus years on the planet and a history of bronchial infections, so a prime candidate for death and/or long-term misery.

The two injections, taken over a month's time, were free.

To quote John Belushi in 'Animal House' – "It don't cost nothing."

Now I would love to think that in a month's time I'll be able to hop in the Camry and scoot up to my local coffee shop, sit there sipping dark roast and taking in the coffee shop ambiance which I have not done once for nearly a year now. Roll into Trader Joe's whenever, shop and mingle freely, not confined to the "senior" shopping hours before the rest of the organic world gets going. Go see a movie, go out to eat at 'Cheryl's' downtown Portland, have breakfast at 'Grateful Bread' in Pacific City. Because, ya know, everyone with at least three still functioning brain cells will have taken advantage of the "don't-cost-nothing-staying-alive-help-save-the-planet" vaccine. Yeah, I would love to think all that. But…….

Can you say "Moron"?

A week or so ago I saw someone post on a social media site the question to their friends and others unfortunate enough to stumble upon that particular web page asking whether or not they were going to "get the vaccine" and did people think "it's a good idea". And people were dropping comments of "I don't know" and "I'm thinking about it" and "No way" and other such medically/intellectually/planetarily goodies. I'd like to be shocked, honest to God shocked. Astounded, thrown for a loop, yell out "I don't understand." Yell it loud. Real loud. Mean it.

But I think I do understand. I've been alive these last four or so years. Unfortunately, I've seen and read and been twittered and heard the news. Herd stupidity. I mean, not only are people actively and consciously choosing not to do whatever it takes to save their own lives or the lives of their children, parents, sisters, grandparents, cousins, foster kids, brothers, neighbors, co-workers, hospital staff, cops, postal workers, youth workers, social workers, neighborhood volunteers, clergy, representatives etc etc etc, but some people for some reason I nearly cannot understand feel it's their duty to keep other people from choosing to vaccinate. Like all those folks who shut down a Dodgers Stadium vaccination opportunity for hundreds maybe thousands of people a couple of weeks ago – all those folks (imho) in desperate need of 15-minutes of Tasing with the Taser dial set on wicked high, followed up with 30 days in the county jail for just generally being an asshole. But hey, that's me. A boy can dream.

There are people in my personal life, I believe, who are considering not getting vaccinated. Maybe have decided not to. That takes me far beyond sadness. Beyond all that understanding I was talking about. Do I consider them "morons" too? I guess, kind of, I do. If not them as morons, this particular behavior as moronic.

I don't know. Maybe it's some kind of twisted live and let live thing.

Or maybe I do know. And I just don't like feeling so sad.

What I know for sure is my right arm aches a little today. And that's a good thing. About that - ain't no doubt.

The Whole World

From the Beach Boys song by that title:

"Late at night I think about the love of this whole world."

It's how I'm choosing to leave this day I was blessed with.

Easy Like Thursday Evening

It's funny that here just after 8pm I just said to myself, "Well, I didn't do a thing today", and yet the facts would bear out that I was busy doing "stuff" and some of it real "important stuff" from the time I pulled myself up from the meditation chair just after 5am until maybe 6pm after I'd set up the kids with their dinners and dropped to the couch to watch Ken Burns' "Jazz" and dream a little dream about all the writing I didn't write and all the drawing I did not draw.

I suppose when my head hits the pillow I may count this - this right here - as doing writing today and if I stand up a second and take a charcoal pencil and curve a sweepy line over the top blank sheet of a sketch pad - there... - well, here's my pillow talk now - "Far out day, Dude."

This is why they say "Easy does it."

Rejoice in It

Let me set the scene. It's the summer of 1987, around then, on the central east coast of Florida - specifically the town of Edgewater, about 20 miles north of Cape Canaveral. Most Monday through Friday afternoons would find me sitting in a small clubhouse on a side street off US 1, there with a bunch of people talking about trying to unscrew-up their lives. I was hoping to do that too.

Summer in Florida must feel like the steam used to turn a nuclear turbine, except more humid - and probably hotter. It's hot. I note what's common knowledge because once or twice a week these two guys would walk into that clubhouse meeting and sit in the back. Both these guys, late

20's, early 30's, were ditch diggers. They dug ditches for a living and mostly by hand in that Florida summer steam bath and they'd come in covered in brown dust with little riverlets of cleaned-off streaks where sweat had slipped through the dirt. You can probably picture that. Sorry, I don't remember their names.

I point out these guys' appearance because there was something striking in the fact that one of those two guys would raise his hand every time he showed up and every time he raised his hand and got called on to speak, he'd say the same thing: "This is the day the Lord hath made, and I will rejoice in it." He said that every time.

Well, it took me a while to get past the "hath", quite a while, but once I did, this guy, both of them, rejoicing in their days, kind of 'no matter what', that began to stick with me. These guys got around on bicycles and I know that because I had a pickup and loaded their bikes in the back in a thunderstorm once and drove them to the trailer which was their home. Them, no doubt, rejoicing all the way.

Last night, Monday night, I had some fairly wicked pain in my colon, I don't really know that, somewhere down there, and I've had similarly located pains rarely but consistently as far back as I can remember. Kind of a Buddy Cushman idiosyncrasy. I mentioned it to Susan, whom I was sitting next to on the couch, and told her if I was scoring pain level on a one to 10 scale I'd give it a two and a half. Shortly thereafter I laid my head down on her knees and we watched a DVD episode of 'Elementary' during which I fell asleep, kind of a ritual for us most nights. When it was over I pulled myself up and there was a new pain, down low in my right side just over from the front and it was wicked, I could barely stand and barely move to rearrange all the books and notebooks that begin days on the coffee table and make journeys over the couch and recliner and get put to bed back where they began. I had the thought I may need to call 911. Then I had the thought I would ask Susan to call 911. Then I had the thought I would ask Susan to put a mask on my face before the ambulance folks hauled me out. Covid and all.

But instead I dragged myself upstairs and moaned a while and sat in the upstairs recliner very quietly and statue-like and slowly and surely the pain subsided. By the time I crawled into bed maybe half an hour later I would have scored it at .5, maybe a smidge higher. Which, the vanishing pain, did not keep the thought from my mind, or, I guess, probably traveling all through my heart and soul, that I might not wake up tomorrow. I think it's a 72 year-old thought. I don't remember having it at 27.

But then I did. I woke up tomorrow - which is today, Tuesday - and after a quick negative glimmer about some minor crap bothering me, the voice of the guy in Edgewater spoke clearly in my head. Crystal. - "This is the day the Lord hath made, and I will rejoice in it." And right then, swear to God, I had a vision of Caspar the Friendly Ghost, the one in the Christina Ricci and Bill Pullman movie, drifting across the room, giving my right cheek a little pinch, and with his big smile saying, "You made it, Bro. You woke up. Again. You're still here."

An hour later I took a pic of myself in the morning recliner, after praying and meditating, after coffees and reading, after looking at an art book, and I posted it on Facebook with the caption "I'm still here." I'd already made a decision, a vow, to rejoice in this day. This Tuesday. Rejoice all day today.

Baby, It's a Letter

(Monday weather)

Rushed to get a letter in mailbox early this morning before regular Monday spiritual retreat. Banged the letter out yesterday (Sunday) afternoon.

I have received only one letter (Keith, LA) in the last year. Oh, sadness. What happened to letters?

That is a koan, my koan - What happened to letters?

I will ponder only this, my koan -- as opposed to idiot democrats and evil republicans hijinks -- the next eight months.

What happened to letters?

It's a koan.

Hundred Thousand Wing Flips

There were small knotholes in some of the old boards, the holes oblong shape, and slivers of sunlight would stream through onto the barn's dirt floor. I was staring trance-like at one of those lit up areas right when I had my first ever true sexual experience, with a girl named Cindy Mawaka. She was 13 and I was 12. It's funny, years later, what you remember – light on the floor, holes in the boards.

Which is all well/nice and though the clock ain't on my heart surely is, timer, like Laura Nyro once sang, and directions fall out and I'm bound to follow, and one of the decisions I've made lately is to cut back on words used per paragraph, at least, and here's hoping sentences as well. As example – When the student is ready the teacher will appear becomes Student ready, Teacher appear. I mean, come on, dig that and possible there is a Japanese Roshi quality to that kind of writing – I wouldn't know never having traveled farther west than Santa Monica or east (if'n I was trying to sneak around the long way) than Provincetown, though I do read Zen books rarely and how I become influenced to the point of plagiarism is well beyond me. Suit up and show up, Brah, I hear tell. (by the way, following my own directives – Suit up show up). Oh, what a sneaky little devil, remove the "and" and the language gleams with simplicity. So, I do have a writing goal beyond simply writing and it is to write more simply, like I explained, and a practice session will look like me turning on the smart phone timer to, say, 15:27 and typing in a rave-on spill-my-guts free-for-all and when the timer does it's end-of-watch thing I take a couple of minutes to get past the rush of welcomed words and then go back with my emotional (and prose 101) hatchet and own and operate "Bendy's Removal Service", it's salad time, Baby, slice and dice. An exciting proposition for 72-year old me, wrinkles and twinkles and all, and I honest to God believe I will grow in personal maturity and plus write way cooler stuff. And who knows how many people ever bother to read anything at all anymore anyway, so less better. (Snuck one in there.)

Now, what about going back to the fun R-rated opening story and try this word-thinning puppy out.

Small knotholes in boards, oblonged, sunlight streamed on dirt floor. Trance-like staring, first sex, Cindy Mawaka, she 13 me 12. Funny what's remembered – light, holes.

Oh hell yeah!!

And

A hummingbird buzzed me today, just over my head, all friendly like, a hundred thousand flips of the wings, and me out staring at a wall of shrubs, still, not perhaps in meditation, but not far from. So there you have it, the super quick kid and the golden oldie out in the yard, possibly fast friends moving on.

(Hundred thousand wing flips.)

Koan #2

I have this incredible group of friends, their number growing weekly, who converse with me regularly and are all dead. Se la vie.

My ongoing corporeal walking around peeps, not so much. I don't hear from them and it ain't me (Babe). I make calls, leave messages send texts send emails greeting cards, words of friendship support kindness enthuse love on and on and get nearly nothing back.

If my current Koan is **What happened to letters?** the first ever created by me Koan, my even brand newer Koan is likely this -

Is choosing a cow better?

Good Timing

I feel I have been trending in the right direction for some time now, on a psychic cellular level, good orderly direction, intertwined among body, soul, and the individual me of me. Something like a to thine own self be true. And digging it.

Body, 72-plus years on the odometer, and mind (all those minutes of living this life), interwoven inseparably. Alchemy. I get that now, a Buddhist sitting on a cornflake thing. Keep it in the day, Brah. Be here now, Bro.

Surely my wife Susan has imagined - and thus created - a space in which I could and have been able to bloom. My unique second-hand rose me. At least so far, up until 6:30 this Thursday morning, 2021.

Gee, I sure hope I serve as a lamp unto the world today. Keenly aware of 'Just this.'

Being

Baby, I'm a rich man.

August '58

It's August 1958 and I'm nine years old. Ginsberg is back from Europe, living lower east side New York, and Ferlinghetti is plunked down in the forests of Big Sur. My dick is getting hard, for the first time ever, once in a while and I dig that. It has dawned on me that, at nine years, digging life is the bomb. (And not the one we crawl under desks from.)

Someone gave my older sister June a typewriter, which she hates, so I've claimed it and have it up in a corner in the attic, right in front of the window looks out on Main Street down the hill. I spend afternoons running through backyards up and down my street, and once in a while drink cokes at the counter and look at teenage girls with short skirts at Water's Drug.

Mostly, honestly, I'm up there at the typewriter.

I think, maybe, I'm a poet.

Take the Bench

Back in '06 and '07 I worked for an outfit called Walden House. This was in San Francisco, most of my time running the adolescent boys' residence in The Lower Haight - '214' - and some of it at the girls' residence in South San Francisco - 'PSK'. Walden House was a California state-wide organization primarily directed toward substance abuse identification, intervention, and treatment. Hardly anybody volunteered to go there - folks were encouraged.

Walden House was an 'old-time" drug treatment program, lots of structure, lots of confrontation, a fistful of slogans. One of those slogans - and I came to know this in the adolescent programs - was this - "Take the bench." Literally the idea was there were benches throughout the building, generally in high-traffic areas - and if one of the young folks (all of whom were ordered into treatment by county Probation departments) was mouthing off, struggling with direction, becoming volatile, some angry adolescent thing, one of the staff would tell them to "Take the bench". And the rules were clear about the bench. Crystal clear. If someone was on the bench they were not to speak and they were not to be spoken to. By anyone. These bench assignments lasted five minutes and the goal, the hope, was that the time would be used for reflection and self-assessment. Best use to ponder "Why am I here?"

Better still was to choose to take the bench without being told, a most worthy option. To have the level of self-awareness that taking the bench - right here, right now, with whatever's going on - is the right thing to do.

In Alcoholics Anonymous, I understand, they talk about "restraint of pen and tongue". Pause before writing or saying something you'll regret. It's good advice, you know, count to 10, take a deep breath. etc etc.

There was something beyond that, though, with "Taking the bench" in 214, "Taking the bench" in PSK. Similar, but further. Some sacred space to ask yourself something like, "Who am I?" and "Why do I do what I do?" "How do I operate?" "How did I get here - on this bench? In this building? Today?"

Pictured above is a bench in the Rhododendron Garden in Portland, Oregon. I've been taking that bench for more than 10 years now, pretty regularly, sometimes actually meditating, usually sitting still and paying attention - the ongoing song of redwing blackbirds, the convoy of duck families floating by. Dragonflies, faraway train whistles. I've made important phone calls to faraway friends on that bench. I've scribbled story ideas in old steno pads on that bench. I've sat with my wife on that bench and bathed and shimmered under the golden glow of true love. Mostly I've sat there alone. I do alone good.

And good for me, yippee, I take that bench of my own volition, my own choice. It's sacred space, for me, blessed territory. And - and I know this - it is not a whole lot different from the bench just outside the program administrator's office - my office - in the building at 214 Haight Street in San Francisco. Honestly, it's not.

Lucky me, I took the bench today. Yes, I could see my breath through my mask, and a few minutes after sitting it began hailing on me.

But, lucky me. I took the bench today.

Just This

My wife transferred me $1400 from our joint account to my personal 'Shares' account today, free government money, earned being a good citizen.

There's a dark grey rabbit hanging out in our yard pretty much all the time these days.

My son in Missouri PayPal'd me a bunch of money I'd lent him back in the fall to get moved and into his new house, ready for the family coming interstate, which they successfully did. My grandkids.

I received a referral from my primary care doctor for a colonoscopy.

I went for a walk early in the 30-degree cold, and I paid attention all over the place and felt physically in a pretty good 72-year-old place when I got home just before 10 am.

I've been reading the 'Selected Letters of Langston Hughes' and read a bunch of that this morning, with coffee.

I watched two episodes of "Bosch" by myself on the living-room couch during dinner - frozen Trader Joe meatballs and an olive salad, 100% chocolate and cashews for dessert, then a cup of Trader Joe French Roast decaf. That was really good. Then I did the family dishes.

My wife's got the couch now, watching a tv show in French, with subtitles. I'm in the basement, here, reporting on the weather,

The Tuesday weather.

Ducks

I heard the hoo-ing of a dove while I was sitting in zazen this afternoon. It was my second sitting of the day, the first at my usual 4:54 am awake alone in the sleeping house, straight back chair with attached cushion in the dark living room. The second this afternoon, in the studio, blessed time gifted to me for a few hours. My zazen lasted 18 minutes this morning, I noticed the phone clock when I became still and again as my eyes opened when that felt right. In the studio I set the 15-minute meditation gong timer on my phone, so no doubt of a quarter hour.

The second sitting, I noticed, was quieter even considering the difference in the world's activity – or lack – between 5am and 2pm. And the attendant noise. The world is woken up and busy with its business and I enjoy some of those interactions, though mostly with wild animals and flowers – like the two ducks, perhaps a 'couple' for life, afloat on the little stream of runoff along the bike trail beside Johnson Creek – enjoy not so much the human kind, though the pre-dawn alone is filled both with quiet grace and missing the wife. Possibly this is a reason for my sitting in zazen now these last 12 or 13 years, to open space for attention, and, I don't know, maybe an aha.

I can tell you, Blog reader, there is barely anything like it, the sitting in the chair on a cushion, the bowing once to the cushion before taking my seat and glancing at a time of beginning. The bowing nine times to the cushion when zazen ends. Even when the racket is wild in my mind, I've come to understand it is not, zazen, scored on how absolutely incredibly yogi deep in a cave still, heart rate down near 40 I become. No, I can arrange and manage and figure shit out about every San Diego Padre game for the entire season, wild diamond mind, and I sit in zazen and I notice all of that and it's good. Quiet. Or. Electric. I believe to sit alone, still, aware of my body, aware of the internal sound, is good.

Like hearing the dove outside the studio and cars traveling the surrounding streets and the creaking of the studio itself, the wood, the roof, the window glass, you know what I mean, old scary stories, the creaking noises of the haunted house, maybe alive and generally not in a good way. Yet, it is what it is. The noticing. The morning is quiet, yes, but me, not so much. The day is awake and busy, though the afternoon light finds me more still.

And....

I don't believe this means anything at all. Honest. Just a simple story – a boy, his chairs, a dove, the Padres, our studio sounds, floating ducks. Yeah, I sit in zazen, every single day of my life since I began back in North Truro on Cape Cod in the April of 2008. How'd I get so lucky, I wonder, never mind amazingly blessedly lucky to still be here – 72 years old and I woke up again today, which, excuse me, Fuckin' A.

But lucky, as well, just sit, do nothing. Walk, see ducks.

Avaians

Oh, to be a better bird.

That's how I flew out from the bed

this morning.

And why.

Rushing, gushing

these ancient joints lubed with a joy

of still can do,

here I go,

these wings,

out beyond the rapacious reaper's ruin.

Ha! Dumb thing,

no match for the avaians.

Inbound dream,

outbound skedaddle,

and this shadow skips along below,

that's me on the roadway,

there and all up here,

mean ole' reaper hafta wait

one more day.....

When

Ima getting up,

suiting up once more.

I'm a better bird,

and all consistent with my whatevers,

repetitious morning joys --

Loop-de-loop

with this lit'n lamp.

And I flew out of bed this morning.

Again.

Clutter

It's 7:35 Friday night. I worked for a youth organization once named 735. Back in Melrose, Massachusetts. Lot of my changes there, the North Shore, all those kid outfits, all the roles I took, all the way up to Director level over and over again. We got good work done a lot of the time, here and there, they call it human services, and I'm thinking it was my inherent business to stress the human. So I'm sitting waiting for a Zoom thing, it'll be in Oakland, CA, where more changes took place and I walked those streets and around and around the Lake, and I got to smile at the races - and mean it - which is one of the real good deals in Oakland. Everyone that's an American ought to walk that Lake at least a couple of times.

I spent some of the hours of the day, this one, Friday, internal weather, rearranging books and pulling out sacred books I've owned 50 years now for donating to free little libraries, around here in Portland, maybe 50 or more in three paper bags, making way for newer books in piles all over, and my wife is off on a three-day silent retreat and when she comes back she'll be happy to see the reduced clutter, and maybe notice I used lemon oil to polish the book cases, and I put all the Kerouac's and Ginsberg's and Burrough's on one shelf, stuff slightly more organized, poetry with poetry, books on how to write better sidled up together, books about musicians together on the landing except Dylan's 'Chronicles Vol 1' over with the Philip K Dick and some other good stuff.

Man, I love books, I love sitting here at the keyboard and over there with a Bic medium pen, blue, spilling my guts in my Morning Pages notebook every morning. I love my pencils and pens and lately I've spent money on charcoal and drawing pads and steno pads and number 8 thick pencils and I'm drawing kitties and cats all the time, there's pulled-off drawn sheets everywhere and I'm having this fantasy/dream/planful thinking that I will collect all those feline creations and create a book of drawings and I know I likely won't sell even one and, honestly, my caring about the investments and devotions of other folks has dipped bigtime.

And maybe all this thinking and two-finger typing and typos I have to stop and fix, maybe this is clutter. Clutter. On a Friday night. Before Zoom. Around Oakland. All these cats. Sacred books.

Travels

Traveling in my mind, today – Monday – I wonder. Do humans flit? As an active verb? Can I?

I am flitting, so's you know, amidst various geographies my precious springtime March, out there in this daylight Provincetown down the way end of Cape Cod, Oakland of course, and a journey of the mind into Harlem with Langston Hughes my guide, though physically I've yet to travel anywhere past those just beyond 110th streets.

There's always hope, I say, and like the mind travel, there are the moments of extraordinary wonder when I visualize the way I'd like it, the where I'd want it. I heard one of the guys in the band "Television" talk about the power of wishes, and, Oh, I do wish for more time, loads and heaps and bundles of time, there is so much good to do, life to be full and wildly lived.......noticed, noticed, noticed -- this, this, now this. Needing to be done. Help this tundra along. And I'm just the guy for it.

"Who dat?" the cats in P'town queried curiously upon the moment of my electronic arrival this Monday morning. But I just smiled, and answered, softly, "The Oregon kid."

Firefly Future

"Hast thou attuned thy being to humanity's great pain, O Candidate for Light?" -- (Tibetan) *Book of Golden Precepts,* ed. H.P. Blavatsky

Yeah, I generally think about that quote two, three times a day. Pretty much.

I came upon it early this morning over coffee, reading Peter Matthiessen's "The Snow Leopard". Which I've been meaning to read a while now, and (Yay) now am.

No doubt "Snow Leopard" will be chock full with questions like the one above, which feels for me within the 'suit up, show up' commitment to living life alive on terra firma. Am I paying attention to the rhythm of this living, breathing planet and the fauna on it? And am I devoted to do my part, shine my little light, be the lamp unto the world, to make it a smidge better? To make a good difference?

My honest answer is, Yup, and this is the right where I'm supposed to be thing. And in addition to me checking in with me doing my part, what I dig the most about the opening quote is the "O Candidate for Light". That's far out. The light I can and ought to shine. The lamp I hold up against the dark.

One of these days - it's possible - I'll become a firefly. Funky fauna.

Hey - Like the song says - "All the world over so easy to see. People everywhere just want to be free." The pain is when they ain't.

Hast I attuned my being.......

March Haiku (American)

Today

Bird feeder swaying. Wren flits, green branch bends - Cool breeze.

(Kerouac offered less than 17 syllables. Said it was more "ours". I think a haiku is how I feel it, letters spilling out from these friendly keys. I chase Wednesday magic.) In 2018 I published my second book of poetry - "Dictation from the Backyard." Within was this spring offering. (#17)

Haiku Spring

I paint a picture, Purple yellow orange blooms, April days ahead.

Reflecting

Chest-pain day.

I see mirrors, everywhere I look.

And I look.

Memoir'd

My wife Susan is working on her memoir. The particular memoir she's working on today. That one. Memoirs are funny, like a pinata, sort of, take a whack and see what falls out, whatever awakes in memoir-ville - any old time and place. So, for example, were I to try and write my memoir it would not have to necessarily cover the time of my entire life, from that early in the morning mid-January in a 1949

New Bedford, MA hospital (thanks Mom) to say a couple of hours ago when my wife and I took an extended stroll through a tree-drenched southeast Portland (OR) cemetery.

That's not how it works. I may choose to write my one and only memoir about the seven years it took me to accumulate my four-year Bachelor's Degree, with time on Cape Cod, time on the Massachusetts North Shore, alive and adrift in substance abuse and bouncing among relationships and a bunch of political actions and activities and leafleting and sit-ins and sit-downs and parades and pickets and the old draft card stapled to The Peoples' Peace Treaty and all kinds of rock and roll and psychedelic brouhahas, and my point is I could write "My Memoir", likely a bestseller no doubt (I'm due), and it would leave 65 plus years entirely ignored and unmentioned. Out of my life. Memoirs are cool like that -- this here is this here time in my life when I was here doing this feeling that and you ought to hear about it because....

Yup. Good old memoirs.

I like the book "The Files of Milky Dent". It's wicked good and if you haven't read it yet get with the program, Holmes. Now that book covers different times and different places so you can't really call it Milky's memoir, though - and this is so cool - there are little memoir eggs and babies and even sperms all through "The Files", so Milky might write a memoir about his time on Cape Cod. Or Milky might write a memoir about his experiences on the North Shore, some of the exact same places I was and so also could but haven't yet written a memoir about. Or, and this strikes me as the likeliest candidate, Milky can write a memoir about "Wonder Pizza", everything about his age-20's time there, being the boss, making the dough, chuckling along with the teenage help, who he gets to meet and the muscle beach guys and life on the Venice Boardwalk and, you see, the whole shebang.

That's what being a writer of a memoir is all about. I peeked at a page in my wife's "in-progress" 'moir and she was making a reference to her childhood at the San Diego Zoo and a cool relationship with something that happened then here in our Portland neighborhood just the other day - Wow!! My wife is dealing from the whole life deck apparently, which, this is my point, a memoir gets to be whatever the writer of that memoir wants it to be and readers everywhere get to rejoice in being able to read about all kinds of wicked far out personal histories and mysteries.

Between you and me - if I was to decide tomorrow I'd reached the point in this life where a memoir was not only called for by insanely necessary, I would pick to write my memoir about the Wareham River. That's my hometown of Wareham, Massachusetts and one of the rivers - the biggest - in it and it dumps down out of Mill Pond, which me and my pal Donnie and tons of fishing tales would be in it, and it floats through town and behind downtown where my Dad was Editor and in front of one of the sections of town where lots of black people live, and I was way lucky to be friends and hang out with lots of those kids in school, and it flows into the water called Buzzards Bay and I will fill my Wareham River memoir with story after story about swimming at Parkwood Beach and Pinehurst Beach and Swifts Beach and being in boats water skiing and digging clams illegally on the Tempest Knob shore and living a fresh-and-salt-brackish-water river life as a kid. Yes, a kid and his river memoir. Maybe my ashes get scattered in it.

See. Memoirs are surely way cool. And unique.

About any of it.

Buddha in the Basement

11 a.m. -- There is a sliver of blue sky broken out and down through the seemingly endless Northwest clouds. Over to the north. Rain devils, why not travel 1200 miles south to Los Angeles where you are needed. They reside here, though, these clouds, so the blue cutting through is a gift. I'm grateful.

Yesterday morning after meditation and during coffee a thought drifted into my mind that I needed to buy a small Buddha, some tiny thing to bring down into the basement, not so much for company – which it would provide – but for some space of spiritual anchorage. This was yesterday, Sunday, and I did go on Ebay and adjusted my desire (the Buddha would have a chuckle at "adjusting desire") and decided on an eight-inch statue, carved and painted bronze, and selling out of Brooklyn, New York. Perfect.

Spending $33 on some such spontaneous vision might seem foolish, or downright near criminal for people homeless and hungry. But there and then, in those Sunday moments – which I never lived before and will never live again – it felt like the next right thing. My wife, in fact, has a stone Buddha out in the yard. There are also Buddhas and a Kwan Yin recreation, and a Native American sculpture my mom pottered decades ago at a job as Activities Director at a nursing home back in the hometown of Wareham, around and about the house here now, plus a very small wooden Buddha my friend Jen in Oakland gave me a number of years back which sometime along the way Susan appropriated and keeps in her car. So, I'm not without a Buddha or two before mine arrives from somewhere off Flatbush Ave, a crow's quick dash from Yankee Stadium. Still.

I'm finishing a library book, I will within the next couple of hours, "The Snow Leopard" by Peter Matthiessen. I have been supposed to read it, I'm sure, at some point during this life and a few days back began. I took it with me to urgent care Saturday afternoon where I had an EKG – nothing wrong here it said – and so much of what's in this book is of my life now which is the same life as the one before my grandparents were born and the same life after the one when I'm gone, and shortly, here in the Monday studio, I will sit in meditation, the gong app set, and both be here now and be simultaneously all over the place and maybe they're putting my Buddha in the Big Apple mail and maybe the sun will find its way through the Oregon cloud cover - maybe it will rain in LA - and I will sit and I will finish my book and I will post my Monday Blog's weather and my heart and esophagus and stomach and colon and left knee and cool haircut will all do their things. Being here now.

My left knee screamed at me this morning, like 5 a.m., which reminded me both that I am 72 and that I am still here, with my very own all-these-years of running around knee(s). Still. And this is just Monday morning.

Tuesday

On a long walk late this morning I saw multiple birds, heard waves of bird songs, aerial lyrics, the winged span of an eagle passing away up-creek beyond my tardy glance. Robins and doves come to linger, jays in squacky conference, I could not say if there's is play or debate or a brand of blue jay jazz. Ducks in flight, ducks on float. The inevitable crows. The morning sun shone warming through early spring clouds, the below-freezing dawn air changed, inviting, I'd say invigorating. For my flying friends as well as myself. And the childhood sound of birds in song gave me comfort and in-the-moment grace.

The remainder of this Tuesday, after the earliest morning rituals of prayer, meditation, coffee and reading, the never-skipped Morning Pages, the pleasure of waking to yet another day - multiply 365 times 72, add some 60 or so more, this grand blessing, all of which I'm aware.......

So when I say much of the rest of Tuesday was colored with mistake and regret, some remorse and glancing blows of melancholia.......well, I can do the math and I do the math, and lucky to be alive doesn't cover it by a long shot. So, if the creek don't rise and there ain't no meltdown and I get to get up and try again Wednesday, well, there you go.

Today Being Today

Wednesday, 7:15 pm.

Today is today. Mostly was today, now creeping along toward a new one. Today is not yesterday. Entirely different, a unique thing. Today is/was unique. Today is today.

I liked today. I hurt my back and both wrists and created general aches and creaks working out in our vast vegetable gardens (Punster) this afternoon, three rectangular spaces none larger than 2x5, two shorter, and one wooden planting barrel. It was 70 degrees and sun-splashed, rare events in the March Northwest. And it was working a garden and prepping for vegetables, joys and blessings, see we'd driven up to Woodstock and checked a few places and ended at the local Ace hardware and were highly encouraged to buy a bag of powerful soil organical improver ($20) and we did and came home and lugged it out back and stripped off winter clothing and with implements including shovel, pitchfork, metal rake, and hand scoop turned soil and dug weeds and added the good stuff and mixed and prayed and possibly chanted (I cannot speak for Susan, I know I did), and after we celebrated by a short drive -- aging, aching body (again, cannot speak for the wife, so this description of me) versus a short walk all stiff and achy and walked into Errol Heights and we saw nutrias and ducks of varying parentage and geese and what may have been a magic goose egg (me) or a rock (Susan).

And earlier I went for a long walk alone which I did as well in the unique yesterday, and made a late breakfast and while eating looked at baseball internet stuff (ditto yesterday) and sat in meditation way, way earlier (same) and drank coffee and evening decaf and I read the same Allen Ginsberg "Journal" book as yesterday and I did a Zoom Oakland thing (today) and yes, the weather was summer-like and sweet and gentle and better today but I still had some raised voice time with my son Spenser (like yesterday) and I thought about my other son Cameron (ditto like yesterday) and about a few friends and about the Red Sox and Padres (yup, yesterday) and I had tinges of electric chest discomfort (like not only yesterday but a bunch of days now) and when we (Susan and I) were walking out of our after-vegetable prepping mid-afternoon walk from the wetlands park - spectacularly beaver'd out - close by our house, she was up in front of me and I was ambling along, I had the quite clear, most distinct, yowser my bowser thought that today was so just today. And so not the million-mile-away yesterday. Which wasn't as cool.

Today being today.

Scavenging

Dust bunnies rolling around my head later here Thursday night. Did some good stuff, worthwhile, support the family, try to stay healthy, a bit quieter today. Daydreamed, on morning walk, about an extended stretch of silence, like four or five days without any talk. Be hard, the wife, the kid, but it's a thought.

These days I tend to save money, some from not a lot, and when I spend it's primarily for used books on Ebay or Amazon and pounds of coffee from roasters in Eugene and Corvallis, both small college cities straight down the 5 in the Willamette Valley here on OR. Reading lots, drinking coffee lots, long walks lots, and hanging with the wife a whole lot. Anyway, a month or so ago I made a decision to splurge bigtime and invested a smidge over $125 for a season of the Major League Baseball network (MLB) coverage. A rather large investment for me. I'm glad I did and the fact is anytime I spend money now it feels like helping the economy which as a citizen is pretty far out. Agree or not - it's real for me.

Well, today was the season opening day for major league ball and amidst the usuals (praying/meditating/coffee guzzling/reading/walking/dancing with the wife/supporting the kid/eating avocados - all that jazz) I managed to catch a few innings here and there, even with the Red Sox rained out, including Yankee Stadium, Milwaukie, Petco Park in my sacred San Diego, and tonight at the Big A in Anaheim taking in a bit of an exciting White Sox team and the Angels. You can never go wrong digging Angels.

These are dust bunny-like facts of a ratatouille kind of day. Here 'cause I promised weekday weather.

Fresh

Twenty-one-minute silent meditation, 5 a.m. Two daylight walkings out in the sweet, friendly air. Blessed. No-sugar chocolate. So good.

This Friday. Let it shine.

Considering Me

I've come to be slightly gentler with myself, over time, and an example is my plan for this Monday afternoon which is drive over to the Cleveland High School track and walk around it either 12 or 14 times, depending on stamina in the moment, track milieu including weather temps, wind velocities, and sunshine-iness, and internal go-for-it level.

In the past, and not so long ago in the scheme and math of this 72-plus year-old story, I would have said walking the track was simply a metaphor for my life – going in circles. I do remember writing that to my friend Bob Zimmerman, or saying it to him, and he passed on to whatever comes next Christmas day in 2010 meaning if I haven't said it aloud or even given it serious thought since, that's a long time. Somewhere and somehow and some ways I have come to look at my life more with purpose, say following some sacred compass kind of thing, the way I call these Monday-thru-Friday Blogs internal ‘weather reports’, well, a vane up there on the old barn roof pointing the way – my path, this journey, now south, back north, way out there to the Provincetown east, and forever west. I believe I was born for the west. That feels right.

So, when I go to the track today and if it is open and the gate not locked and available for some intensity of meandering – call me Ole Man River – I will know, in heart and mind and soul – I ain’t just heading around in circles, Bro, no, no way, every single spin again, 440 yards Baby – will be unto itself, each go-around a come-around its own – special. And if I’m paying real good attention, and I tend to these days and its been better for a while and see, that right there, that’s big old gentle me with me – well, you get to wake up in the morning after all these 72 years of days, you still get to wake up and the knees still twist (and shout) and, okay, shake it up Baby, and I begin to see everything anew, well, that for me is being blessed.

And there were a lot of years where the word “blessed” wasn’t in my vocab and now I do not pass a day without it sometime spoken or thought, so, again, I’m on my path and it’s moving forward, ahead, even when it feels like reverse, sometimes, so, like I said, this is me being gentle in my (own) mind. With me. For me. Considering me.

So Young

Beach Boys, “So Young” alternative take, post dinner dishes, Allen Ginsberg piling up in on-line book carts, it’s all about the war Baby. Like the song says, “…Then Mama’s baby will have seen the last of me.”

I'm about the transcribing, Holmes, the story telling, documenting the moments, we share in ways and we change by our own seeing. I me mine. There's a pile of books over there on the cabinet in the basement, all my unsolds, must be nearly a couple hundred. These were recordings, like the Beach Boys, alternative takes, and tomorrow I'll zoom the Oakland cats and tomorrow I see my young son catching vaccine number two if'n he don't make it too big a thing, in his head, beforehand, unlike how the Beach Boys sang "So Young", showed up and do'd it, real similar to the way I document these passing weekdays, like that movie with all the college grads and their beyond college lives, "Just tryin' to keep the conversation lively."

I kind of like doing the dishes, sun going down, early evening bird song, cleaning the counter, cleaning the stove, water in the coffee pot for tomorrow so early in the morning, it's one of these nights, here, now, where the crazy words might spill out endlessly. But like that pile of books, who would want to read them?

Coming to My Census

I jerked up and out of a coma-like sleep in this afternoon's recliner, I'd been reading "The Letters of William Burroughs", wide awake and meanwhile as well to the accompaniment of two cups of Allen's Corvallis coffee, four bags arriving in a box in the mail today and one freshly opened and perked and heavenly, and well, the coffee I think is part of the story – these brief stories I cutely refer to as my daily weather, and which I share with y'all Mondays through Fridays.

So I'm wide awake and reading this most interesting book

and quite suddenly I'm jerking up, I sense I've been far away, and I might be hallucinating weasels rushing around the living room and past my lifted-off-the-floor recliner feet, and is that a rapping on the door, and I have this instant thought that out there on the porch is Dick Nixon collecting our house's information for the US Census, him having been sentenced to a couple of hundred hours of community service – for the stuff he did – and if you're young you can look into it through the world-wide web. But, just moments later I begin to come to my senses (census) and it comes to me I may have fallen into an immediate and crazy heavily mystical sleep, from the wide-awake reading moment, and the very next thought is this is a coffee thing, which if you think about it the idea of stimulating coffee with its caffeine sending me into this coma doesn't sound logical, but see I do have this theory that I love coffee so much – which I really do – and love being love, all strong and powerful and with great powers, the coffee crush has caused me to become entirely warmed and fuzzy'd and it is this warmth and fuzziness which has relaxed me to the point of crashing beyond any degree of unconsciousness 13 seconals ever left me in. If you can dig that.

Then again, these days I always have to take a look around, often out of the corners of my ancient eyes, to see if the ole birth certificate is laying on a breakfast counter, on the rug in the midst of rushing weasels, out there on the porch with the Tricky One, or here in the kitchen, as I clean the old grounds from the pot and can't help but begin dreaming about the sweet brown liquid tomorrow so early in the post meditation a.m.

My birth certificate – Jokester.

See, this is me…..coming to my census.

Show and Tell

This photo, Thursday, taken just after 8am, in my car. See the three – it's show and tell.

Left to right – That baseball, familiar baseball stitching, that baseball has traveled with me out and about, hither and thither, a big hunk of my life. Found in the infield of the track at the old Wareham High School (no track there when I was a school-attending kid), this Saturday mid-day I'm the only one at the track, I've left a meeting with a bunch of local cats in the town hall basement, folks getting together and shooting the breeze about fixing up their lives, and it ends at noon and I stroll over to walk in circles a while, this before continuing my travels from up in Lowell to out onto the Cape and visiting my mom who has recently suffered an aneurysm of sorts, her brain, and is recuperating, and me down, like every weekend, to visit and offer whatever comfort her son offers, and I want to walk on a track new to a particular physical ambiance I rejoiced in as a kid as part of the journey. And on the grass is this used baseball, and I have cargo shorts and stick the ball in a pocket down one leg, and I'm guessing this is like 2002, could be a couple years earlier, and the ball goes into my Taurus and rides with me down to the Cape and back to Lowell and later in a move to Medford and over and over again down to the Cape and I carry it when I walk all over, and I move to Berkeley (CA) and then Oakland and work in San Francisco and the ball goes with me and in my shorts when I walk the circumference of Lake Merritt and quite possibly the length of the Crissey Field path by the Golden Gate and its with me over and over again walking the Cape Cod Rail Trail after my Mom has passed and I work in P'town and run an HIV/AIDS house and live all over and it travels with me across the Country again (3rd time) out to here in Portland and these last few years it tends to stay in the car. These connections. Around a gifted baseball.

Those cards – on top couchsurfingat70.com – well, here you are, and I had those printed and I took that photo from the rooftop of my best pal's apartment house three blocks up from Lake Merritt in Oakland, above the six floors and I went up there a bunch of times over the years when crashing in his studio and I loved the view and I loved this pic and it right away felt like the couch surfing visual. Its spirit.

"Grace" – My wife Susan created this, in her studio, sculpted clay, energized with love, devotion, hunger to make it all better. "Grace". Who'd of thunk me carrying around the word "Grace", man you can travel back through my life and lots and lots of folks would get a good chuckle over that. There's the then and there's the now. Way less chuckling. It's a word which came into my life maybe 20 years ago, back when I was traveling to see my damaged mom. Back when I found the baseball. These days I begin every morning on my knees, on a cushion (old knees) and among other prayerful requests I ask the Great Spirit to fill my day with Grace.

The Great Spirit does.

A baseball. A couch-crashing rooftop. A promise.

This is show and tell.

Empty

Friday night empty.

Colors

Purples, pink, pale oranges – sunrise paints. My Morning Pages written, perhaps a smidge more somber than other mornings. Still – just waking up is a victory. And I laugh out loud with my reading and coffee, following 22 minutes in the meditation chair. I may be a Buddha (Buddy-a) but I sit with my feet on the floor.

There's some blood in the toilet – more morning color – and changes in plans moving forward, including a Zoom with some folks in Oakland, a large crew and mostly African American. I feel at home there. Like my hometown, white and black, even more colors.

I continue to make plans. I've paid for four nights at the coast next week, all-alone retreat, and Susan and I scored tickets Saturday for accumulated-miles-paid round trips to San Diego for a week-long August adventure. Making plans is good. Holding, generating hope and new hopes, is good. Aches and pains, unwelcome color where there ought to be none, well, they are what they are. Like the palette of today's sunrise was what it was.

I've woken up and I have paid pretty good attention and I have been a strong participant in life. I also stamped and licked an envelope into which I wrote a letter to my best friend yesterday, and which I plan to walk to a faraway postal box later this afternoon.

See, more plans. Coloring my world.

Nothing About Nothing

Six days from now – exactly 38 years ago – I met a guy named Frenchie. He was a longshoreman from Charlestown, MA, retired, a bad back, and he traveled all about the greater Somerville vicinity with a couple of cats named Eddie G. and Jack.

By chance having stumbled into this trio, and in those days without a lot to do, I began running with them. That generally looked like meeting in the Brigham's Ice Cream parking lot on Broadway and getting in Eddie G'.s car. Those guys spent a lot of their nights going to and speaking at what you might call 'self help' meetings. They told me – the kid – it was good for them. They said stuff like, "You've got to give it away to keep it."

During the years I continued to hang around I must have heard each of them make their little speeches 25 times, at least, and every time it was Frenchie's turn up there at one podium or another he always said the same thing – "I don't know nothing about nothing." He never didn't say that.

People generally would laugh when Frenchie would say the 'nothing' thing and for two years I thought he said it to get that laugh. At the two-year point, and after more get in the car rides than I could count, I began to believe that he, Frenchie, really, in fact, believed it. He truly believed he didn't know nothing about nothing and was simply telling it like it is.

Five years after I met Frenchie and began hearing his 'story' I called my best friend Bob Zimmerman, out in El Cerrito, CA, and when he picked up the phone and said "Hello" I said "I'm the thin man." He said "Who is this?" and I said, "It's me, Bro, and it's dawned on me that I'm

Bob Dylan's Mr. Jones – the Mr. Jones of 'Something is happening here and you don't know what it is. Do you, Mr. Jones?' Like I don't know nothing." I believe Bob's reply was "No shit."

I haven't thought that way much these last 33 years. I don't think about Frenchie too often. He and Eddie G. and Jack all left us long, long ago. Bob Z too. But this morning, this Tuesday, when I woke up and ached myself down into the meditation chair and onto the coffee and reading recliner, I sparkled with the certainty that, for me this Tuesday and like Frenchie always said, "I don't know nothing about nothing." Not today.

Nothing about nothing.

Old Saying

A few people I knew long ago use to say that if you walked into a room full of people and everyone had thrown their troubles in a pile on the floor, you'd be lucky if you grabbed your own when you left.

What do ya think?

Wednesday.

April

What Eddie C Said

I am usually 'Mr. counting my blessings every 10 minutes'. Paying my best attention – as the Buddhists say, noticing, noticing, noticing – and taking note of how gorgeous the day and planet can be, is in fact when that is where as a species we all go. A guy I knew long ago, Eddie C., a guy who helped me out a lot in the growing up and not taking myself too seriously and the blessing counting department, he use to say, "As long as I don't pick up the first drink and work on taking care of myself the best I can, it's impossible for me to have a bad day."

That was a hard one to believe back in the late 80's, early 90's, but he hung with a crowd that said if you want what we have you do what we do, and I hung with that crowd too and I wanted what he had – especially that no bad days thing – so I tagged along and listened most of the time, and more and more as the second hand swirled the circumference of the clock and weeks and months and years passed, I moved closer to that "no bad day" place.

Today was an anniversary of sorts – 38 years way back to my last drink and my last drug. I think there is some connection, maybe an itty bitty one, between the want we we have and no bad days crowd and the abstinence thing. Then again, there are days when I don't know nothing about nothing.

It was amazingly beautiful in Portland today – sunny, high 70's, balmy and Spring blooming out all over. I got to wake up again and pray on the cushion for a grateful heart and sit in the meditation chair with my swirly and usually gentle mind, drink a few cups of delicious coffee, walk in the wetlands, and even play a little baseball with my son. If Eddie C. was still around he'd be saying, "See, Buddy,

I told you. You don't pick up the first drink and you try to do the best you can and you get these days and they add up and become cumulative and your brain fissures and synapses dance around, you get new eyes, and, told ya, No Bad Days."

I'm still trying to do what he did and get what he got. Because, truth is, I'm not there yet. Not this sunny day.

Bell Tell

Not really, good old Bell Telephone, but it's a phrase I remember and pretty much the only company you got in the ear-to-ear, handing on the wall, 20-foot curly cord so as to be able to walk around the kitchen and prep dinner or prep the dishes or scramble some eggs and drop the toast in the toaster – all while talking. The good old days of long telephone cords.

I'm not much of a telephone guy. Them mobile now, smarter than me – way smarter. Chips, cameras, Netflix in the coffee shop upholstered chair. All that. But, in terms of using the thing to dial and call another human, not me so much. I'm thinking we are all "built" in our own unique ways – the bozos on the bus thing notwithstanding – and I'm just not built to be a telephone kind of man.

So, today, Friday, has been an outlier. Early this morning, strolling the front door street, I called my sister Nancy in Wareham, Massachusetts. Long time no call. Later in the morning I called Sandy, my older sister, somewhere down there winding down the Florida 'snow birdy' thing before heading back up to Manchester, New Hampshire. While on the line with her I saw a call coming in from my number one pal Gavin in Oakland, CA and not having the high-tech skills to answer a call when on another, it was 45 minutes later before we hooked up. And an hour or so ago, 1:40, while on a walk up to Reed College and back amidst the abundant sunny warmth, I called Butch, my high school neighbor and often time running buddy and active friend over all these last 50 something years. He was listening and offering a listener's comfort from the shoreline of the Florida Panhandle.

Each of these calls lasted a long time, in fact way longer than I generally do or (even) can tolerate. The audio speaker option helps, though mostly I use that to play Beach Boy songs while on walks. Today I used it to share what and how my life is today, this middle-of-April Friday, and hear their thoughts on how it is – my life – today.

It helped.

Alexander Graham Bell – yeah, I guess the guy had his moments. Plus, and he'd have liked this I bet; we get cool screen savers now.

This Week's Posts

Some of the Monday through Friday posts here the coming week will reflect internal 'weather' I experienced last week. I will try my best to remain true to the day in which I am posting.

Little Did I Know

I had a mentor of sorts I'd found back in the early 80's – this cool gay guy who was helping me out with the whole don't drink and drug thing. He was forever telling me that there was "a plan" for me, that my Higher Power – whatever that was – surely had a plan for me. A good plan, all about caring for me. That plan. One day I walked up to him and asked, with attitude, if my High Power has a plan for me why don't I know what it is? Then Dick, that was his name, looked at me with his sweet, gentle, grinning smile and answered, "Because if you knew what it was, you'd fuck it up."

When I began this Blog – couchsurfingat70 – back on August 7th in 2018, I choose the name 'couch surfing at 70' because it felt kind of cool to me, and because I intended for the Blog, unlike my previous 'BuddyCushmanArt' Blog which was a lot about politics and current events and often angry, to be more of a place for stories, mostly my own and as well from those I'd observed over the years – over the decades.

And it, the new Blog, was in fact related directly to years – my rapidly approaching 70th – and my ongoing daydream about spending time with this friend or that one, like I'd been doing a bunch of times with Gavin in Oakland and had with Andy and Jamie on Cape Cod before Portland. It felt funky, in a good way, being 70 and still willing and able to live that couch surfing, nomadic, gypsy-like life.

Little did I know.

Someone once told me that the only real guarantee in life was that if you didn't pick up the first drink you couldn't get drunk. I could dig that, seemed like night following day, and it's worked for this boy for a smidge over 38 years now. It's just I guess I forgot it was the only guarantee. Because it felt like a guarantee – to think otherwise unimaginable – I would live the rest of my life with my wife Susan. Since the day I met her – September 24th, 2009 – she was my life partner, she was my soulmate, talk about fate and you're talking about us.

Last Wednesday, the day before that 38th anniversary of sorts, my life partner and soulmate told me she wanted a divorce. To say I was stunned, well, I was stunned to my core. I seem to have forgotten the "no guarantees" thing. Maybe it's shame on me. Maybe, like they say, it's life on life's terms.

It's Susan's house. Me getting out was part of the deal – stated. Is part of the deal. Little did I know, back two and a half years ago birthing this Blog, I would find myself in the position of possibly relying on couch surfing again. Even, maybe, to the point of survival. And the surfing now with a tad less romance – not quite so funky.

I sure wish Dick was still around, because I'd call him up today, this afternoon, Monday April 19th, and I'd ask him, again, about being sure my High Power has a plan for me that involves me being cared for. Because I know, for sure, what his answer would be – "Guaranteed."

Then, after a moment or so, he'd give me – I swear I'd see it right over the phone – that sweet, funny, caring grin of his, and he'd be the one asking the next question:

"Why, are you fucking it up?"

That B

I just got back from a pre-surgery nasal swab Covid test. It, the swabbing, kind of tickled. Tickled is good.

On the way to the medical center I was listening to The Byrds. On the way back it was the Beach Boys. Last night looking at a Padres/Brewers baseball game the announcers got talking about the Boston Red Sox, and one noted that on the 2018 world championship team the three outfield members were Mookie Betts, Jackie Bradley Jr, and Andrew Benintendi. The so-called Killer B's.

The Byrds, the Beach Boys, Betts, Bradley, Benintendi. That's a lot of B's. I'm Buddy, another B.

Another B is "Be Here Now", at least the verb of it, and I cannot speak for anyone else but lately it's been all I can do but to be here now. Asking what I experience as my Higher Power to help me understand the will for me for the next five minutes – only five minutes – and on my side of the street. What's the will for me the next five minutes on my side of the street?

When I first long ago began hanging out with the don't drink no matter what crowd I was often advised to "Ask for help." That's what you did – you didn't drink just one day and you asked for help because, surer than shit, you were gonna need it. I slowly learned how to do it, the ask for help thing, and – like I said – these days it's pretty much just for the next five minutes, and the wondering what's going to happen next. And asking for help. Lots of help. I surer than shit need it.

Be here now. That B.

Tweet, Tweedle-Lee-Dee

In his book "Cat's Cradle" Kurt Vonnegut Jr. has a line which says this:

"Strange travel suggestions may be dancing lessons from God."

I read that book in college, along with most everyone else, maybe late 60's, early 70's. That line pulled me in from the get-go:

"Strange travel suggestions."

"Dancing lessons from God."

I think – and I am not sure of much these days – but I think one of the gifts of life is pretty much everyone gets their own mind and gets to figure, puzzle stuff out in their own unique way. So, everyone who read "Cat's Cradle" and wasn't speed reading and came across that line would have the unique experience of understanding it his or her own way. All of which may simply be an unnecessary paragraph.

Travel suggestions can come – me thinking again – in any number of ways: verbal suggestion, overheard conversation, note blowing in a breeze down the lane and slapping up against your right leg, orders from the boss, a line in a book. Your wife saying she wants to have a talk.

I received a strange travel suggestion one week back, strange mostly in its unexpectedness…….no – its inconceivability. But there it was and it involved the necessity of actual travel because required leaving of home was implicit in the suggestion.

Two mornings ago, alone in the house, (not having hit the

highway just yet) my son sleeping in his room, me finished with meditation, on-the-knees prayer for a grateful heart, two and a half cups of coffee later, and having sat in the 40-buck recliner purchased upon first new life in Portland – January '09 – sitting and waiting for something, well, a dancing lesson I think, after all that I stepped out onto the front porch. On the railing, four feet away, maybe less, was a robin. It turned slightly and gave me a look. But it did not fly away. (And for all I know right then I could have been a strange travel suggestion.) It sat on the railing, eye to eye with my stillness and silence, my hush these last days.

The robin had a twig in its mouth. Maybe I should have said that first. It had a twig in its mouth and its eye on very-close me and I swear the thought came over me that you gather twigs to build your nest – robins do – and just possibly there may be times when robins get sent to make the suggestions, those strange travel suggestions. Maybe this robin.

"Yo, quiet boy, time to make a new nest. It's what you do when the old one's gone. You go gather the first twig and you push on from there and you might not know, with that first twig, where you're going to build it. Just that you need it and no one's going to build it for you and oh, by the way, we – those of us of the orange persuasion – we do it one twig at a time.

It felt like a dancing lesson.

With a Little Help….

"No man is a failure who has friends."

If you are like me, and kind of stuck on the holiday movie

"It's a Wonderful Life", you know that is what the angel Clarence writes to George Bailey after dramatically showing him he, George, had indeed lived a wonderful life.

I bring this up because a little less than a week ago, after receiving unexpected and pretty terrible news, I began a daily series of long walks on a sun-dried path between two rows of trees. Thinking. Daydreaming. Sobbing at times. Reflecting.

That's a good word. Reflecting. Here I am 72, about to be homeless and pretty much without direction, and I'd called my friend Gavin in Oakland a couple of hours after I heard my life was less wonderful than I thought, and I called Gavin because he is my back and forth, give and take, laugh and cry, buddy and partner, one-time boss always asking for my guidance and all the while teaching me non-stop. Someone you call, someone who calls you. Let's you in on cool music groups. An old-fashioned best friend.

And on those walks I got to thinking that Gavin is the only friend, like that, I have now, at this time in my life, 600 miles away, and there are people I know and before Covid sometimes hung out with, coffee and stuff, here in Portland – one called me Tuesday – but it was not like that, not like with Gavin.

One friend. That's what I thought. You're 72 years old and you have one best friend. And I cried when I thought that and into my mind came the word "failure" – I swear it did, failure in the 'human' department – and Warren Zevon's "I never thought I'd be so lonely this far down the line." That was me, maybe last Friday, walking, and thinking……… reflecting.

Then I posted on Facebook my new reality and many,

many people showed up to offer consolations and hang-ins and you'll get through this's, and a couple of Portland people offered direct help and I have taken them up on it in tangible ways and it has eased my burden, and especially regarding my son Spenser and safe passage and harbor for him.

Then yesterday, a latecomer to the comment gallery, a man named George, one of my old high school pals I remain in connection with after more than 50 years, maybe he'd just seen my post, whatever, he added a comment. This one: "Buddy, you've had many challenges in your life. But, you know, you have far more friends than most people I know, especially friends that you have kept all your life. It's hard to get through times like this, but you will, and be stronger and better for it."

I cried some when I saw it – thank you George – and this morning on yet another of these endless walks I remembered back to the fall of 2005 when I was leaving Medford, MA, and my job as a Program Director for a youth agency, heading off for a new life in San Francisco, off to live the dream, children, follow my bliss, I remembered back then two different people, one a therapist and one a friend who hung around with the don't drink crowd, both women, they both in the course of a couple of weeks said the exact same thing to me. Verbatim.

"You have no idea what you mean to people."

George says I have more friends than most people he knows. Far more. Dana and then Mary said I didn't have a clue what I meant to people. I think, I guess, perhaps I'm not such a good judge of myself, my real deep-down self, as I stroll and bounce along through life, something of a Gypsy and in fact in love with that image in my head, even if it means, like Kerouac, I see myself as a "Lonesome traveler."

I did not see myself that way these last nearly 12 years, not one single day, and yet my very best friend in the world, my soulmate, is gone. But meantime Gavin has called me every day. Every day. And someone has offered me a place for the month of June, bartered for a couple of paintings, so I can spend another month with Spenser and support his transition to his new "traveling" life. Someone else has offered me storage space -ditto bartered for art – and maybe enough so I don't have to pay a self-storage business, because the truth is every single dollar I've got or can get is a lot. Dana and Mary, back in '05, were saying "Don't go….people need you." And so many people have phoned in, on-line, these long last few days and said Hang in Bro. We got you. We got you.

No man is a failure who has friends. That's what Clarence wrote George. A week ago I had the thought maybe I was a failure. I do not have that thought today.

Thanks to my friends.

True Love Ways

In all my life I have never felt more than right now, right here today, that it is my life's work – my true path – to sit at the keyboard and rave on.

Rave on, Brah.

Say it.

There's A Lot to It

I can see it like it was yesterday. Summer into fall, 2007, the sun is shining, the days are balmy, welcoming. The Red Sox are winning. There's me, crashing on a loft bed wide open above the kitchen of my sister Sandy's house. Her house along with my brother-in-law DeeDee. Yeah, he's got a more 'formal' name, but that's who he was – to me, to everyone who loved him. A whole big bunch of people. DeeDee.

So there we are, we're in the living room, David, his son, is there, Jordan, his grandson, is there, Sandy flitting around the house doing something. I'm couch surfing having left a job in San Francisco and a couch-surf with my friend Gavin in Oakland and just driven across the country with my son Cameron, who flew out for that experience with his dad. By this time, in this story, Cameron's safely back in Florida with his mom and at least three of us boys are watching the Sox – well on their way to another World Series championship – me a month short of a new life down in Provincetown running an HIV/Aids house. And something is going on in the game, or something isn't, and there's a lot of noise in the house, or there isn't, or the Cape Times paper's open with one or another gruesome headline, or not, and maybe it's between pitches, but DeeDee turns from his recliner and looks back at me and says this – "There's a lot to it."

I knew DeeDee from probably early 1970's on and through my leaving for Portland – 2008 – and I cannot remember the number of times I slept over a month or two – and in all those years and all the dinners and shared yard work and talking about one of his kids or putting me to work on one of his house-building job sites, I cannot remember anything he said to me more often than that – "There's a lot to it." Sometimes he'd embellish it with "There's a lot to it, Kid", which I kind of liked, the youthful thing and all, and he'd say it within the milieus of craziness, sadness, trauma, cracking up laughing, not taking himself serious at all – within any and all conditions.

There's a lot to it.

Lately DeeDee, and him saying his saying thing, has been on my mind. However else it might be said – "Life on life's terms"; "Shit happens"; "The bitter with the better." Like I'm rolling down the highway, it's one I'm all kinds of comfortable on, and then there's a fork in the road – "That was never there!", I yell, and some unexpected turn, some detour, some big-ass change of plan is required, and the only thing you can do – the only thing I can do – is make the turn. And see where it takes me.

And in that last little story DeeDee, back from heaven and back because the planet got smaller when he left it, anyway, in this last story DeeDee is magically sitting in my back seat, he's just there, quiet, watching, and I come to the fork and I have to take the turn and I do because my road – my path – has changed and I drive a few hundred feet.....slow, and I turn around and I look into the back seat and there's DeeDee, that sweet smile on his face, and he reminds me, "Kid, there's a lot to it."

The Next Right Thing

I've always liked that saying, from whenever I first heard it, I think maybe with the don't drink one day people, or it could have been in one or another residential setting with some loopy adolescents. Don't remember. But I always liked it, with its implicit action of course:

Do the next right thing.

Lately it's become a mantra of sorts for me. Now what? Now what? What's Next? Now what do I do? Why – silly goose – do the next right thing. A mantra for me as of late because my universe kind of got sucked into a black hole a couple weeks back and I came up for air with – like Dylan – no direction home. No "Home James" for this cat. Just a Now what?

They say to keep it simple. They say take it one day at a time. It's all good stuff and there have been a lot of days in my life when I have lived a little better, more fully, even, maybe with a bit of righteousness, following those suggestions. But those days aren't these days and these days I've been sitting and staring off into the space of a living room I've spent my early mornings in 11 years now. With a blank sheet of a steno pad on my lap, balanced on one leg, wait for it, Buddy, wait for the inspiration and jot it down and then you can go and make one of your "To Do" lists and start checking stuff off. And one could make a case that that, doing that, going down the list, is doing the next right thing.

But generally, breathing again isn't on the list. Generally, repeating what the deal is, the real deal, over and over and over again to your son, the one with the "condition", in the hopes that on the 11th or 13th time maybe it sinks in, maybe some of it, nah, that's not down there on the list. Asking for help from the Higher Power thing for some understanding just for the next five minutes – just that. Not down on the "To Do" list. But, for sure, at least I think, in the moment the next right thing.

There are important things to do – as important as life gets, and there's also letting go. There's looking for boxes and there's selling things you've loved the best you can love things because, well, it's a thing, and it's right, and maybe it's what you do next.

Lately I've been doing a lot of what feels like the next right thing. What feels inspired. What feels shared by that "Power" space, for me the breeze blowing down the street. What about this, Buddy? Here's a thought, Buddy.

They, those people I told you about earlier, they also say first things first, and that feels a bit closer to doing the next right thing, and reminds me my friend Donnie Sisson from my hometown days saying, "All you can do is all you can do."

Pretty much all I can do – am doing – these days is asking for help and hoping I'm doing the next right thing. Which, I think, is a good thing.

What Johann and Joe Said

I think it was this past Friday, out on one of these real long walks I've been taking twice a day the last couple of weeks, a thought came to me, each word clear in my head, the thought resonating through my entire being – soul and all.

It was this: "Give all my energy and love and devotion to the people who are supporting and encouraging me" I know that's exactly the thought because I was close to what is still my home and ran in and grabbed this old notebook which I've been using to write what feel like inspirations during coffee time in the early morning, and wrote that thought verbatim. There's nearly four pages filled so far with those early thoughts, there's self-advice, To Do's and musts, and the this be your life now, Brah, statements of fact.

Implicit in the give **all** my energy thought, I hope, because it's crystal clear to me, is giving every smidge of my energy, love, and devotion to my encouragers means not one iota of attention or nano-second left for the discouragers. Not one moment.

Here's an example. Suppose I go over to my Facebook page right now, Wednesday afternoon from the basement, and joyously share that today, within the reality of my marriage broken, the air sucked out of my universe, technically homeless in a few weeks, in the midst of those emotions and tears and facts, I'm posting that, with nowhere to go, I have decided to live pretty much a lifelong dream and so I'm going to move to San Francisco. Worked there almost two years, but never lived. I never would have imagined this reality, my life right now, but here it is, so that's what I'm going to do.

An hour after posting eight people have replied.

This from the first seven – "Are you kidding?"; "You can't be serious."; "Do you realize how expensive San Francisco is?"; "You're living on social security and that's it and you think you can move to Frisco?"; "More typical Buddy delusional thinking."; "There's no way that will ever happen."; "Are you fucking crazy?"

Then the eighth person chimes in – "That's totally far out, Dude. Man, that city has your name all over it, The Beats, the Airplane, the Haight. The ocean. Bro, I can already see you sitting in some Market Street coffee shop, that goofy grin on your face, joyful in just getting another day, never mind that day's in San Francisco by the way. Buddy I can see you strolling, no, Brah, I see you skipping down the path through Crissy Field, I know you love it there, look, there's Alcatraz, there's the Golden Gate right fucking in front of you. My man! And you know what? I got you Bro. I got you. I'm there for you. I'll help."

The first seven people won't exist in the world for me. They just don't. This is me, Wednesday the 28th, saying I will love with all my heart the people who tell me I can, and give no more of my time to those who want to convince me I can't. I'm past my 72nd birthday. I'm about to be homeless. I just can't afford it. I cannot waste the time.

Oh – the headline to this post. Let me quote from a couple of cats who have been zooming around within the world wind of my life long and rather sweetly now. I, for sure, can see them hanging with reply-er number eight.

"Be bold and mighty forces will come to your aid." – Johann Goethe

"It is miraculous. I even have a superstition that has grown on me as the result of invisible hands coming all the time – namely, that if you do follow your bliss you put yourself on a kind of track that has been there all the while, waiting for you, and the life that you ought to be living is the one you are living. When you can see that, you begin to meet people who are in the field of your bliss, and they open the doors to you. I say, follow your bliss and don't be afraid, and doors will open where you didn't know they were going to be." – Joseph Campbell

Think what you want. Rebounding off a supernaturally painful breakup and bouncing into something so stupid. Perhaps. You might say that. But if you do, I won't be listening. I'll be over there, just right over there, with the "Yes" guy. Trading dreams. Trading lemons for sparkling water.

Supposed to Be

Back in the early eighties I had a mentor kind of guy named Dick M. That was his name. He was one of those don't drink just today folks, and as he was indeed a mentor to me, I guess I was (one of those folks) too. I sure liked him a lot, and he seemed to like me.

Here's one way I could tell he liked me. Periodically, like every two or three days, I would stroll over to wherever he was, drinking a coffee, talking it up with some guys, hanging out with the woman he hung out with, who was not his girlfriend or anything like that, more of a special lady friend. Anyway, I'd walk over and he'd turn to look at me – he had such a gentle, kind, and caring look – and I would begin with some complaint about life's unfair and why me and I don't deserve this and where's the benefits for all my hard work – stuff like that – and Dick would widen that sweet smile of his and almost always say the same thing. This thing:

"You're right where you're supposed to be."

To be honest, it wasn't my favorite answer. I was leaning more toward "Poor Buddy" and "I feel you" and "Yeah, life can be so unfair", predictable kinds of answers anyone would want and expect, that's what I thought then. But, no. "You're right where you're supposed to be."

Two weeks ago yesterday my wife told me she didn't want me anymore. She told me she was filing for a divorce and, this being her house, you need to go. The first thing to come into my head was not "You're right where you're supposed to be." That advise-type-answer didn't show up. Trying to catch my breath showed up, and walking out into the world and calling my best pal down in Oakland and sobbing and crying and asking for the comfort of his voice and the wisdom of his words, all that showed.

Since that Wednesday the calls have continued, daily, most from him to me, some from me to him. I've spoken with a couple of other friends, and received gifts of tangible support. I have dived deeply into the world of Zoom and spent an hour or so many times a week sitting with more of those "Just for today" cats. And kittens. This morning, zooming my way down to Oakland, with mostly people of color looking back at me, someone asked if I had anything to say. I said yes, and I told them about a guy named Dick M and what he'd always say. I told them that wasn't what I thought of when I received the "This is the end" news.

You know what else I told them? I said that after all the phone calls looking out for me, after all the people asking how can they help, after every morning me on my knees asking the Great Spirit for help to have, once again, a grateful heart, and sitting in meditation every day in the straight-back chair and letting in nothingness, endless and empty – after morning coffees with open pads and notebooks scribbling down every idea slipping on into my head, and some pretty wild ones – kids – about where to now? and how many writers do you love who lived off couches and kindness and electricity for the typewriters? – after all that and a lot more, I told them that this Thursday morning I had the feeling, pretty clear, pretty believable, that, well, I'm right where I'm supposed to be.

It Felt Like Friday

Emperor Wu of Liang asked the great master Bodhidharma, "What is the main point of this holy teaching?" "Vast emptiness, nothing holy," said Bodhidharma.

"Who are you, standing in front of me?" asked the emperor." "I do not know," said Bodhidharma.

The emperor didn't understand. Bodhidharma crossed the Yangtze River and went to the kingdom of Wei.

Later, the emperor raised the matter with his advisor, Duke Zhi. The advisor asked, "Majesty, do you know who that Indian sage was?" "No I don't," said the emperor. "That was Avalokiteshvara, the Bodhisattva of Compassion, carrying the seal of the Buddha's heart and mind."

The emperor felt a sudden regret and said, "Send a messenger to call him back." Duke Zhi told him, "Your Majesty, even if everyone in the kingdom went after him, he wouldn't return."

I've read this koan many, many times before, in John Tarrant's book "Bring Me the Rhinoceros." While I was out walking this early afternoon it came into my head. It felt like Friday.

Me and Fats

It's hard.

Some days are hard. I woke at 3 a.m. and could not fall back asleep a long time – whirring and swirling, wondering, wondering – and I fell asleep at some point and woke up into this Monday and my thought was, it's hard.

Last night, on a walk, a friend I don't talk with a lot called and asked how I was doing. I get a lot of that these days and I am grateful beyond descriptive language for each one and, the fact is, it's helping to hold me up and keep me taking one breath and then another. Last night's call, however, was different from everyone I've received since "the news" two and a half weeks ago. Every other call I've received – every single one – has kept the focus on me. How you doing (Buddy)? How you holding up (Buddy)? How are you taking care of yourself (Buddy)? How can I help you (Buddy)? Not one has had a word – not one word – about my wife.

Until last nights. That friend went off on my wife with a bunch of stuff I won't say here. Along the way I was advised I'd be a – quote – "fucking idiot" if I did not take better care of myself…..in a larger sense.

The call ended and I felt a deep sadness because I have never once had any of those thoughts and I don't want to have them. I may be a screw-up and a less-than on any number of levels. But I can look in the mirror and see an old guy with a good soul. And I have been trying my best to make the next decision, and lift the next box, and make the next right move directly out of my soul. These last 18 days. Because that's what I want and because that's who I am, and because – wherever I land – there's always another mirror.

The friend who called me last night had my interests at heart, I know that. I'm grateful for the call, if not the fallout. Part of the 3 a.m. wide awakeness, residue of divorce and heavy sadness, some ongoing disbelief, and I suppose just a smidge of anxiety when the next "now what?" rolls in.

Today, before I woke up, the "To Do" list was already filled, long and challenging, with all kinds of "separation" business – separate the car insurance, separate the phone billing, change the health insurance paying – and much of it involving more money for me to cough up, money I have some of but would rather not spend, me in fact selling most of art canvases and my bass guitar and bass amp and my Squire guitar and Fender amp, and my easel and my art supplies because – cold, cold world at times – like my former brother-in-law Deedee, who you read about here last week, was also fond to say – "Money talks and bullshit walks."

Me and Fats Domino walking. And I cannot speak for the Fat Man, but today's been a little harder than usual to keep walking through.

Whatcha gonna do when the well runs dry? Hope for another call, I guess.

It's 3 p.m. Monday.

Dumpster Divinations

In the mornings I think about stuff. With two or three coffees, and even more (thinking) lately since I stopped reading three weeks ago. Can't get a grip on the words. So, it's me and coffee and three steno pads and one wire-bound notebook, a Bic medium pen, and whatever random thoughts stroll in, float in, whisper on in, barge in, those that sing to me, they all go down in their allotted place and most mornings I go back and re-read what I've been writing these last 20 days and it helps me to complete the ritual and head down to the basement and write my Morning Pages and other early morning necessities.

The other morning, maybe the end of last week, working on what feels like some synaptic connection between inspiration and common sense, I realized that I needed a place to throw away a whole bunch of my paintings painted these last 10 or so years which I consider nice try but no skippy. Probably about 20 of those. On our street – well, on my wife's street – trash collection is limited to one gray garbage-like barrel and just twice a month, and anything beyond that costs extra money and the wife (who had me served "papers" by a neighbor yesterday), anyway, the wife has made it clear to me I can't be running up the bill. So, onto a notebook page I wrote I need to find someplace for all the stuff I'll be discarding and letting go before June. Including those paintings.

Yesterday morning, Monday, I walked out very early, maybe 6:15, onto the front porch and looked to my right and down about four houses, snugged up against the sidewalk and taking up maybe a third of her (the wife's) street was this industrial looking dumpster, like you might see on a construction site or in some petro-chemical warehouse district. I thought "hmm" to myself. Later in the day, in one or another of my daydreams, I saw myself sneaking out in the middle of the night, my arms overflowing with no-longer prized works of art, and just as I'm about to flex up and throw everything over the side flashlights and floodlights come on from everywhere and I can't even get out of town right. As in, do not pass go.

This morning, in one of the steno pads, I wrote "Ask the neighbor if you can throw your paintings in his rented dumpster." So, charged with extra oxygen from a couple of deep breaths, I walked down the four houses and interrupted a garage conversation between people I've never met and said, "I'm from four houses down and my wife and I are separating and I have about 20 paintings I need to throw away with nowhere to throw them and I was wondering if I could throw them in your dumpster?" And the guy I've never met said something to himself about it probably won't add much to the weight and looked at me and said, "Go ahead."

It's easy to feel like a victim. It's easy to wonder "Why me?" To ask the Gods. Lucky for me about four decades back I was introduced to the idea that there was some power, some force in my life, that had the goods on me and – in spite of that – had my back. Always had my back. Had my back even when it all seemed like a shit show. A number of people have reminded me of this fact the last 20 days, and, me myself, well I've moved a lot closer in touch what that power, the one I ask for help for a grateful heart every morning. The one who has me still here – up above however sad the ground is. Some cat with a plan for me.

Like a dumpster down the street.

Out of the Closet

My son Spenser and I began this afternoon the work of cleaning out his closet. For the upcoming move. Like some crash sale – everything must go.

Regular readers of the Blog likely know Spenser has Down Syndrome. Which means his thinking process is unique and works just fine for him except when it doesn't. Like being told everything must go and hearing the reason why

– which he played no part in – about 100 times (so far) and saying he gets it and saying yeah, let's do this, and saying we'll be okay, Dad, and saying no way, saying un-huh, you're not touching any of this, saying it's staying right here.

Where it's been the last four and a half years. Today, after watching him eat a lunch I made for him and watching "Dickie Roberts" (a favorite of us both), and just before convincing him to take a between-rain walk, I was able to bring him back to an "okay" with the packing-mind-place, and I told him I'd bought heavy-duty trash bags when I did his food shopping this morning and I brought them to his room and said I could start loading the likely 150-200 t-shirts piled on the floor and in boxes and a clothes hamper and the mostly-fallen down closet hanging bar and he said, no, he wanted to do it. So, I stood behind him holding the bag open and he took his shirts one by one, slowly, and dropped them in the bag and I asked every once in a while, was he sure he wanted to not bring that one to his new home and he'd say no and drop it in and I got teary because this is just too much some time and my son, my son who you could say doesn't always get it but sure gets loving his t-shirts, he's paying the price of the adults. And after a while the bag was heavy enough and I kept reminding him he and his new family could go any time to where all his shirts and DVD's and all his sacred stuff will be stored and he said one bag was enough today and put the things back that had been in the way, and then we went for a walk and came back and he sat on the couch to watch "Deal or No Deal" – the couch where he loves to sit and watch the smart tv and has all these years and that's coming to an end and I'm not sure he really gets it. And I came down here to the basement to write this – what I call my "daily weather".

This is what they glibly call "collateral damage" in war and other violence movies. And mostly he doesn't really get it, and he sure doesn't deserve it, and all I can do is help him walk through it – the easy part, moving in with people who have worked with him for years, and who love him – and the hard parts, like his beloved shirts, one by one, out of the closet and into a bag.

Keep on....

I saw I'd received a (disturbing) text from my wife last night – who was two rooms away when she sent it – and I said to myself don't read it right before bed (9:30) and I read it and alarms and crazies and fears and emotions went off in my head and I was up and stayed up and waking up through much of the night. And I decided to write about it here in detail, all through the night I rehearsed – and then I decided not to.

I've heard it said that your Higher Power does for you what you cannot do for yourself. That is, if you believe in that sort of thing. I do, and there's much evidence lately and sometimes it's as clear as a bell and sometimes you (I) can't see the forest from the trees and sometimes it works like "this sucks" and "why me?" and down the road – what? Two days? two weeks? Two months? – sometime later, upon reflection, speaking for me, it's like I'd of never got here if there wasn't a "there" and yup the "there's" lately hurt so bad.......But – still, there's that doing for me what I can't on my own, and they also say there's a plan for me, if you believe in that, and way back in '84 Dick M, mentor and cool guy, said I didn't have to know the plan, when I asked why I didn't, and if I did know, he said, it I'd probably fuck it up.

And those proceeding two paragraphs are likely just rambles, my this Friday version of letting it all hang out, and I've received great, sweet news and offerings today and potentially really bad possibilities close ahead today and maybe things are being done for me I can't manage on my own, and I bet in fact there is a plan for me about which I'm mostly clueless, and back in the day – my Wareham High School and Cape Cod Community and Salem State days – we were fond to say "Keep on keeping on." And I was just upstairs packing books I cherish into boxes headed for storage and who knows how many miles from where I may land, and making lunch for the kid, and recycling all kinds of things that mattered a few years back but not so much today, and I'm not feeling the thank God for Friday thing because it means another day has come and is going and the end of the month is closer and this right here will all be over and gone and, so, what else can a 72-year old cat do but keep on keeping on.

All I got.

Kindness's

Henry David Thoreau said the kindest thing a human being can do is to allow another human being to help them. Maybe not in those words exactly, but that was his point – be kind….let somebody help.

Those don't-drink-one-day-at-a-time people have, I'm told, a saying which says this – "You've got to give it away to keep it." Yes, not a twin to what Thoreau said, but no less than a second cousin. You get back when you give.

This is not karma discussed here, I think far beyond the reaches of karma, and likewise removed from the what goes around comes around thing. More like a neighbor down the street.

Thoreau's words ring most clear, and they shimmer with goodness, and human possibility and potential – to be humane. The species which thinks. The phylum – if I have that right – which makes choices. Say "Yes" when someone offers help and you have bestowed a special kindness to the offeror.

I've been thinking about what Thoreau said because I've been in a position this last little less than a month to be the recipient of one offer and act of kindness after another. It's been a bit mind-blowing for me, and the truth is my first inclination with a few of the offers was to slow down, tap the brakes, and say why don't we think about that. And in those moments, I have forgotten that to be kind is to say Yes.

Someone I've met on Zoom, a guy in San Diego, called me while I was walking Saturday morning, he was checking in on me, how you doing? and all that caring, and I mentioned a couple of these offers and he said it was a duty – in this case my duty – to say Yes, that to do otherwise would diminish the experience of giving for the other. And when he said that it resonated as exactly right because I know it's right and my hesitancy to accept the kind offer has something to do with a "not deserving" piece of baggage. Which leans into not good enough (or maybe bad-off enough) and now 'damaged' (but not as damaged as that guy under the bridge), and, I guess, something of a self-esteem thing.

On another walk last week, one night, talking with my friend Gavin in Oakland on the phone – he who I called the day I heard the word "divorce" and the one who has called every day since then to – in fact – hold me up and pretty much save my ass. Talk about kindness. Talk about giving. And on that call on my night walk last week I told him that someone had messaged me and told me some people from my old high school days were talking – about me – and decided they wanted to set up a "Go Fund Me" account for me. And my right away action was basically "Nah", there's people so much more deserving, and in need, and Gavin said something like, "Dude, they established that fund for people exactly like you – lost a spouse, lost a home, selling your important things for rent money, technically homeless in a few weeks. Why not say Yes?"

I did end up saying Yes, and more recently continuing to say Yes to other seemingly over-the-top offers of support, some of those Yes answers moving past the initial "Oh come on" to the understanding that through this sadness and fear, and through all the amazements and the worries and the dreams of some new path, crazy, day-dreamy things, somewhere walking along this new path I remembered what I'd read so long ago. Maybe in "Walden". Maybe something else he wrote.

The kindest thing I can do – now, these days – is say yes and let somebody help me who's offering to help me.

And, I think, to feel worth it too. I think that's part of this path.

Recycled Me

Monday's a recycle day on this street. This street in Portland, Oregon where I magically appeared some 11 years ago, and from which I will leave one final time at month's end. I admit that the water's around me have grown, and the times are a-changing.

Anyway, sometime late morning or early afternoon the recycle truck rolls to a stop and sends out it claws which grab and flip the blue recycle container up and over, its contents fluttering down into a growing pile ending up where I have no clue. But, not some landfill, which is the point, which is important and good. Yesterday, a Monday, the recycle container belonging to this house was heavier than usual, and chock full.

I spent much of Sunday – Mother's Day – pulling Spenser's t-shirts and miscellaneous paraphernalia out from the front of his closet so I could get to the multitude of boxes and bags I had dragged into this house those 11 years ago, and, it turns out, most of which I've been hauling back and forth across the country and one Massachusetts town after another for the majority of the years of my life. I was able to be in Spenser's closet for a bunch of hours without him losing his unique mind about me touching even one thing because I'd arranged for a two-night overnight with his real-soon-to-be new family. That's smart social work, ease the transition of such an abrupt coming change – and smart self-preservation, allowing me a slightly less emotional move-out experience.

Except it wasn't. I pulled out box after box and with my large recycle bag at arm's reach, went through all the papers and letters and awards and fiscal threats and come-ons and bring-downs and memory after memory of most of my life. And, with rare exception it all went into the bag, and me and the bag went out a number of times to the recycle bin outside, filling up with bits and pieces of my past little by slow. But steady on. And I do not say this with ease or in any way glibly – it hurt and broke my heart to throw (recycle) many of those things away and there were a few I just could not – but mostly I did. Because I've got to go and I've got to take every last bit of me with me, and I say that not angry or feeling like some powerless victim. This is simply my story today. Clean out the closet, Bro.

One of the pieces of history I came upon Sunday was a browned and faded copy of a section of the New Bedford Standard Times, which was the area daily growing up, and on the front page of the "local" section were pictures of a number of area July 4 parades and right there on the top right corner was a picture of the Wareham parade – my hometown, – and my mom all dolled up in some historical outfit – looking radiant and beaming and happy. My mom was not always happy and she passed away back in 2005, but she looked joyful that day so it felt like this very big Mother's Day blessing and gift for me. Truly. And after a while the Standard Times went into the recycle bag too, and then on to the recycle bin.

My Camry will hold only so much stuff – the stuff of my 72 years – and a friend has let me trade my art for her garage for storing paintings and precious books, my meager collection of furniture, and those bags of Spenser's delicately collected and dropped-in t-shirts. The things of my life that I have sold and donated and given away and thrown out – and recycled – this last month would shock even me if there had not been a moment one morning a couple of weeks ago when I saw myself writing in my notebook, "It's okay. It really is okay. There's a new life now for you and it's okay to let the old one go." And including the "stuff" of that old one.

The old one with pictures of my mom and letters from past girlfriends and thank you cards from staffs I've supervised and nurtured, graduation photos of my boys, and both paid and unpaid bills from various states and all the stuff I've been writing here about letting go of this last month.

Once Spenser is settled and safe and "living large" once again, I am okay with not knowing what's next for me. Hell, eight weeks ago I was in urgent care with electrodes checking chest pain. Like the man says, there wasn't no white chalk outline around my body when I woke up today, so something good's coming. For sures.

If you are a regular reader of my Blog, thank you. These days you're getting a recycled me.

Do-si-Do

On a walk last night I got to thinking about yin and yang – yin-yang. In fact, those three words have slipped into and through my mind a number of times the last few weeks. To be honest, I've never truly understood their meaning or if yin was the 'good' one and yang the 'bad', or vice versa, or maybe good and bad has nothing to do with it at all. In the organization known as Al-Anon there's a saying which is, "You have to take the bitter with the better." I suppose that is kind of the way I've thought about yin and yang all these long years – one (don't know which) stands for 'the bitter', the other 'the better.' But, again, I doubt that's it.

I googled yin and yang a few minutes ago, here on a Wednesday morning before I leave to go pick up my son

Spenser from a three-night overnight with his new 'family' and bring him back to his room – his own room – now depleted of the desk and bureau, his closet nearly empty, a high mound of boxes and bags and t-shirts by the window to be gone through for saving or 'deleting', and hoping he's mostly okay — so I googled the phrase or saying or whatever and after reading the prime definition I still do not have any clarity, something about the yin femininity and shadows, the yang passion and growth. Something like that.

All I can say is that for all the years of my life since I first heard those three words together – yin and yang – and I'll take a wild guess and say it was sometime in the sixties, I've felt it meant that life had its opposites and quite often they traveled through the world arm in arm, inseparable partners, offering both comfort and ennui. Pain, maybe, too. So this dramatic one-month-exactly-now change in my life, which initially and lasting a while was all one or the other of them – the pain one – has also do-si-do'd around to something else. Somethings else. Like someone I have never spoken with before yesterday saying, on a phone call last night, that even despite such a heart-breaking life situation, maybe I am – he said – on "an adventure." It's a word which has come to me the last couple of weeks too.

Having no address, come the 31st, also means having no address. No yard to sit in, no lawn to mow? No place to call home, no other place unavailable. Not good examples at all, but they do and have for a while rung in my head – and it feels like in my soul too – with a sense of the yin and yang thing.

If someone had told me, say, three weeks ago, "You can end your marriage and leave all those responsibilities and set off in your "twilight years" to who knows where on some amazing "adventure" I would not have given it a nano-second's thought. Never in a million years. Go read through my books of poetry – the poems I have written and shared. The truth is there. But then life do-si-do'd me and there I was and here I am and slowly through this last month lighter patches of wonder and possibility have slipped out from behind the terrible, scary storms and clouds. People have helped.

And that sense has felt a little yin and yang-ish to me. However that goes.

Briefly

Late to the keyboard today, most of which has struggled past. I'll be brief.

This has been a wipe out day. I was wiped out, fully, by 7:30 am, where I could be found at the basement table, weeping over my then-unfinished Morning Pages. Earlier, at 5:30, I'd read two texts from a former college colleague and fellow trouble-maker, the first of which encouraged a look at legal action and protecting my rights – a path I have shied from – the second a reminder that in the ways of this big world I am "a senior" and seniors have protections and services available and opportunities for help with housing and food and even legal assistance. I look in the mirror and I don't see senior and go on my walks and don't think senior and in my chronic daydreaming I remain a kid, both at heart and within my world view. The big old world. The big world in which the birth certificate says – yup – senior.

Then a brief talk with the wife. Then a second, a bit longer talk with the wife, in the basement, me with pen in hand over the Pages, and these were the first two talks at all since the word "divorce" seemed to fall out rather easily a month ago. And I went for a long walk and had some breakfast and watched "800 Words" and did some packing stuff and Zoomed down to San Diego and woke Spenser at 1pm and made his lunch and we watched a Cinderella movie with Selena Gomez and went back up to his room and he was a real champion – amazing and steadfast – reminding me the sooner we get this all packed up and cleaned up he can move up to Gresham with Aaron and live with his new family. And it didn't hurt. It felt great, he can already see something else and he's excited and he'll get to live with way younger and way hipper and way more energetic people who already know him and love him and their world has become and will become his world and it fills my heart with incredible gratitude. Talk about angels.

And after a while we played whiffle baseball in the back yard where we've played for years and I think I'm more aware that's coming to a quick end than he is, which is good, and I've sat out there these past few weeks with bigger eyes – like Lindsey Lohan says in "The Parent Trap" – Making a memory. And then the wife, who has taken off her ring but I'm keeping mine on cause it's my only jewelry and I like how it feels – the wife and her daughter drove to Five Guys and got foods I no longer eat for the three of them and I ate some stuff out of the refrigerator which I've helped pay for and ate in the basement and watched another "800" episode then went for my second walk and realized I forgot my phone and couldn't call Gavin, and the fact is my body hurt all over today and my nose bled for no reason this morning and my spirit quivered some, and I said this would be brief and here comes the trance of my finger dance on the keys, but it's late and way later on the east coast where this morning's text came from and lots of big, big support these 30 days and if you've hung in with this Thursday ramble so far, thanks. Maybe I'll do better keeping it simple tomorrow.

....

My computer was hit by a trillion virus-like intrusions today. I kept being kicked out and away from the things I was trying to do – scary "Fatal Error" blue-screen messages and no cursor to be see, I had to manually shut the computer off then turn back-on, try to recover the Word docs and this very Blog site and important other things and bang, it would happen again. After a while I ran a couple of cleaning programs and a defraggler someone had installed (whatever defragging is) and that takes forever so I went away and only now have come back (4:30) and I'm here so something must have gotten better.

If only that was the worst of it. My problem de jur. Like regular, normal life stuff. Flat tire, bat in the attic, returned letter you forgot the stamp, cable out, overdrawn debit, stuff like that. No, the bigger stuff. The way more difficult stuff. The life upside down stuff.

When I fled the defraggling computer I went for what I think will be the first of two walks today. I did the walk I've pretty much always been walking this last month, down to the tree-lined middle of the road dirt path up to Reed College and back, probably two and a quarter miles, and I had on the to-do list from this morning's time in the recliner with coffees and steno pads to make two morning walk calls. A friend and one-time co-worker back on Cape Cod, and a guy who lives in Florida who grew up five houses from me, meaning we've been friends for 66 or 67 years, and in touch sooner or later all along the way. When I called the guy on Cape Cod who'd texted me, he'd just heard about my month-long problem de jur, the upside down one, and he was devastated he said and please call him tomorrow which was what I did on the walk today, and we were 30 seconds into the call when he told me he'd received an emergency call from the cops or medical people at a local hospital last night – right after his text to me – and that his son had been rushed in —– and passed away shortly later. Tears came to my eyes and I said I would hold him in my heart – the way folks have been holding me – and he left for the funeral home and I had (with myself) the conversation about "You think you've got it bad, it's just a marriage, it's just an address, it's not this." I flashed on both my boys.

Five minutes later I called my childhood friend and I told him and he said it was truly terrible and it also didn't mean my going-away marriage and going-away home weren't also terrible and painful and drenched in sadness. Life on life's terms those don't-drink-one-day-at-a-time folks say. It all truly sucks my friend said. After a while we finished our call and I walked home and did some packing and Zoomed into San Diego for an hour and did more packing and then Spenser and I did some in his room and we had our Friday weigh-in and I drove him to Subway for his dinner and then I came back to the basement and the computer was working enough for me to write about all these troubles – little ones and the others, the ones which ache down deep – all the way.

And that's all I have to say. It's Friday. If the creek don't rise I'll be back here Monday. Please stay safe, and hug everyone you've got to hug.

Running Empty

If you're older, like me, you probably remember the Jackson Browne song "Running on Empty". It came to my mind in the recliner this morning, second cup of coffee dwindling, notebooks askew, and when the song arrived I knew through and through there was not a thing metaphoric about it.

These days (another Browne piece of music) I'm doing something I was forever doing in my 20's and 30's, well my 40's and 50's as well – Moving. Like the riding the bicycle thing, do it, learn it, it's imprinted forever. Kind of comes naturally. Except, now, there are 72-year-old muscles doing the packing and discarding, lugging and hauling, the recycling, up from the cellar, down from the second-floor, over from the studio, out to the down-the-street dumpster, out to the trunk of the car, the back seat, the passenger seat, all available floor space. Moving, moving, moving and the muscles having to move as well, though not with the grace of a, say, 27-year-old. And certainly not with the strength and stamina, and no doubt there is scientific jargon to describe the dwindling capacity of a forearm or a tricep to do forearm and tricep things they once did, when life was maybe a bit more casual and recovery was a given, and not a wish.

Yesterday, by 7pm, I was exhausted. It has been building this last month and the big, big weary caught up after the after-dinner walk. Physically, emotionally, mentally….even spiritually. Not that my spirit has waned – no – because the truth is my spirit feels electric and attentive and, most of all, blessed. Like Gavin said the first afternoon through my tears – there will be bright edges to this darkness, Bro. Nah, last night I wasn't tired to the point of falling down in the spirit. It was all the rest of it. And shit, I've had it pretty damn easy when we think of the troubles people can have and do have day in and day out.

But the birth certificate, that giddy old piece of paper signed sealed and delivered back in New Bedford, Massachusetts in January of '49, it was the certificate having a chuckle at my expense, and everything hurt and there are dings and blood patches and scrapes and cuts and lower back screams and knee spasms and I barely see the tangible get-out progress though there's been much, and the road – that great road Kerouac sung so sweetly of – the one which whispers "Get yourself up and at 'em, Brah, there's a whole new world waiting, you could never even have imagined it, even with all your chronic daydreaming and your life of bouncing hither and thither." That road seemed distant last night, far away, because I had come to the point where I was running on empty.

And, it's cool. We gotsta do what we gotsta do, right, and the alarm went off at 4:35 this morning and I got up and prayed and sat and drank two and a half coffees and along the way Jackson Browne showed up – a little after the fact – and I wrote my Morning Pages – every single day since May 2011 – and I've been packing and lugging and went for a long walk and talked for a long time, twice, on the phone with two different people I have never met or spoken a word with before while on the dirt-between-the-trees walk. Because there's a lot to it, including magic, and there's a lot to do, and that road, which today sings just a little closer ….."Buddy….."Buddy",,,,,it's waiting and so's the industrial-sized jar of Ibuprofen.

Seeing, Believing

Late afternoon, empty mind, dust in the nose and down the lungs, serious Spenser room diving in – him the "Star", me his "employee" – now late and nothing here (Couchsurfing) yet and the promise, the vow, of M-F posts will be kept, and I was thinking of Dr. Wayne Dyer, who's cassette tapes I began listening to way back in the early 1990's when I was living in Lowell and running a kid mental health residential program in Quincy, and if you know eastern Massachusetts that means a direct pass through downtown Boston, every day twice a day, meaning there was a lot of time to listen to cassette tapes, and there was a company called Nightengale Conant which produced such things on mass and I was trying to be better and do better and think better and live better and I was a daily devotee of 16 sides of good ideas in these slick rather large plastic cases, and Dr. Dyer had a couple I was fairly bonkers for and I was thinking half an hour ago, wrapping up in the kid's room, that I was in a semi-hallucinatory state and was probably seeing stuff, and I'm believing some things these days, and I remembered Dr. Dyer used to turn that "seeing's believing" thing around and would always say "believing's seeing", him explaining on tape that if you believed enough and long enough and strong enough and purely enough in something – yeah, something dreamy – that eventually you'd see it. Like a dream come true.

And I have about four of those large plastic cases from back then I've unearthed with all this last month's moving process, and they are going on a "free" table I plan to put out front Saturday, and in the trunk of the Camry is a Les Brown case ("Any day I wake up and there ain't a white chalk outline around my body I know is going to be a great day.") and I'm going to keep hanging on to that

30-something year gift from the mystic, I dig Les, and lately I've been doing a whole lot of the believing thing.

And waiting on the seeing.

Dusty Glimmers

Strung out, busy, dusty, and productive.

Not in a bad way.

The kid's shining today too.

This Wednesday.

Judge Joe Will

Sometime early in the 1990's I was living in Florida and working in Deland as a "Delinquency Case Manager". That was a formal, human service-y name for a juvenile probation officer – employed by the State of Florida. At any given time I had 20-30 kids on my caseload, almost all of whom were good kids in court for being kids and being screwy and a tad stupid – and a few likely already had a bed with their name on it up in Raiford.

Two or three times a week I'd be in court presenting a written report, sometimes called forward before the bench to explain something I'd written and advocated. Every once in a while there was a mean judge in the Deland court. No sense of humor, a short supply of tolerance, and easily agitated in the legal sense. Most days, though, the person in the black robe up on the dais behind the bench was a guy named Joe Will. Judge Joe Will. Young, easy going, a positive demeanor, a good listener, and, oh, tolerant and with a good sense of humor.

The rare occasion when Judge Will's affect slid into a darker realm was when the same kid was back before him for the, say, third time in two months. Or when a kid was yawning when being given a break. Or turning around and making faces at his friend during the middle of the judge's explanation of the immediate facts of life. Or before him because they (he or she) was profoundly blowing off his/ her parents, to the point of abusiveness. On those occasions I would watch as Judge Joe Will leaned forward ever so slightly up there from behind his bench and said words to the effect of, "Son (or Young Lady), the next time I find you standing here in front of me in this courtroom, you and I are going to have a "Come to Jesus Meeting."

Maybe that's a common enough phrase – a come to Jesus meeting – but I had never heard it and I began hearing it often enough that it kind of imprinted itself on my brain. To the point where I would use it myself here and there over the rest of my human service career – and on occasion with a family.

The idea of a "Come to Jesus Meeting" has drifted into my mind the last week or so. It was there this morning, in the recliner, with my second cup of coffee. As a question to me. Is it the time for a "Come to Jesus Meeting?"

I vowed, after I'd recovered sufficiently psychically and physically from the word divorce, that my leaving of my marriage and my home these last 11 years would be with both grace and dignity. Nothing else. Brokenhearted but not all-the-way broken. Devastated but opening, every day, to help…getting what I need. And doing it, I honestly feel, with grace and dignity. Now I understand, here this

Thursday, where the “meeting thing” is coming from – lots of hard advice and shared opinions from friends and acquaintances about taking better care of myself. Me with a lot of through-the-night awakeness playing scenarios and conversations in my mind. Enough so as to the point I’m surprised not at all that Judge Joe Will has strolled back into my world – this five-plus week world – me with a whole bunch of not knowing what’s what. And with what those don’t-drink-today people call “Letting go and letting God.”

I’m feeling my way along, sometimes through the dark, trying my best to be someone with grace, someone acting with dignity, no matter what. It isn’t clear to me, here and now, where the other stuff fits in between and alongside grace and holds hands with dignity. Or if it doesn’t. Look up “Clueless” in the dictionary and there’s my picture.

Judge Joe Will was a real good guy. He invited me to lunch once. He chewed me out in open court another time when my court report recommendation for a young black kid who’d been caught firing beebees at street lights be a 1000-word essay on B.B. King. I thought it was cool, Judge Will not so much.

Anyway, this morning Judge Joe Will came to me to say “Hi” and I said “Hi” back and that’s all I can tell you.

Guarantees

I got on a bus in Laguna Beach, CA New Year’s Eve 1982 and hopped off in downtown Boston at the Park Street station four days and 96 hours later. A guy named Bob was there to pick me up and take me back to his apartment in Medford for what I hoped would be an extended stay. Couch surfing. The thing was, I was placed in a room with lots of baby decorations, the nursery, and exactly two days later Bob took me aside and gently said “You gotta go. The baby’s coming.”

Fortunately for me my little sister lived about four miles away in Somerville – just outside Boston – and a phone call to her produced a couch for me, graciously and with sweet welcome I might add. I said I’d like to crash for just a little while. I left in August. By then I’d found a job with kids and gotten sober and found an apartment in Somerville to call my own. My little sister had saved my ass, giving me time and space to begin to ‘get it together’.

About four weeks ago, actually the day was April 16th, I called both my sisters – who love my wife – and told them about the divorce word, and they both expressed deep sadness for me and – here’s the thing – my little sister, now living back in our hometown of Wareham, she said she had an extra bedroom and if I could handle her dogs I was welcome to it.

The same old song – 38 years later.

I know it’s 38, without doing any math, because the day after the divorce word I celebrated 38 years without a drink or drug, and I began that journey a few months into the time on my sister’s couch. Back in those early days I would on occasion run into the don’t-drink-just-one-day crowd and some of them would talk to me, give advice even, and one of the things they told me repeatedly was that you may hear a lot of things from us, but there’s only one guarantee – “If you don’t pick up the first drink you can’t get drunk.” They guaranteed that,

They did not guarantee that all the packies (liquor stores, cherished Massachusetts word) and bars would close to aid me in my sober quest. They did not guarantee I'd hit the Megabucks or that little children would run before me in the street, tossing flower petals over their shoulders to welcome my way. They said it would be "A life second to none" but they did not guarantee that meant no troubles, no pain, no failures – no heartbreaks. They did say the life second to none would be filled with joys and wonders I wasn't capable of imagining the days they told me of it, that life. Yes, I may find the girl of my dreams, they said, and find we were soulmates. They did not, though, guarantee that girl would love me always. Or not send me away. Just don't pick up the first drink, they said, and you won't get drunk. That we guarantee.

Just a smidge over 38 years later my sister was once again offering me shelter from the storm. This time, a week or so after the offer, I graciously (I hope – the grace thing feels most important now), I graciously said thank you but no thanks. I think I'll try something else. See what else this life second to none – which I have indeed had and have to this very Friday morning – see what else there's planned for me.

Just suit up and show up. They said that too.

Technical Difficulties

The keyboard on which I'm typing this Monday morning sits on the old Cushman kitchen table from when I was a kid living with my parents and two sisters in Wareham, Massachusetts and which my mother gifted to me some 50 years ago and which has been hauled and motorvated and delivered back and forth across the United States more times than I have fingers, probably, and here today sits on four legs on the basement floor in the basement of the house where I have lived and loved and had something of a life renaissance these past nearly 12 years and now about to come to a sudden end. Beneath the table sits my desktop, goofily sitting on the floor since I came down from my second-floor writing room when Spenser showed up nearly five years ago, and this morning I am mentioning this keyboard under which my fingers are dancing (my two index fingers) and the desktop computer (Lenovo Professional) on the floor because in less than two weeks I will have to disassemble all of it and hopefully fit everything – including the rather big-ass monitor directly in front of me on my growing-up supper table, and hope I can remember which wire goes to which input spot and I hope I remember to take pictures of where the stuff is in the back of the computer, the speaker wires and monitor wire and power cord and then pics of the surge protector because it's got to go, all of it, when I go.

And for the next month, or less, beginning June 6th, most likely, when I vacate Nehalem Street for good, I am hoping to reassemble the Lenovo on a patio in the house in the next town over belonging to someone I met early on in Portland when I was running a respite foster care program and she was a therapist-like person for badly screwed-up kids and a few weeks back she agreed to a June extra bedroom space for me in exchange of two paintings – ironically the extra bedroom which I have seen one time has already hanging on its west wall a painting I painted many years ago and which Kate bought – I remember doing the exchange of canvas and cash parked on Belmont Street in front of the Rockin' Frog cafe where Kate liked to meet me after I'd gone on to another job and then another life with a new wife.

So, anyway, the point here this next-to-last Monday morning in May, is that maybe I don't put things back where they belong and maybe I can't get her internet signal out on the patio and it's on this computer where I write this Blog Mondays through Fridays and on which I have written most if not all of my eight books, so if I can't get it up and functioning I'll be left with the newer Dell laptop on which I Zoom (it has a camera, the desktop don't) and basically nothing else, all of which could mean this – "Technical Difficulties". But I hope not.

My plan is to try and write and post one of this week's "Couch Surfing" posts on and from the laptop, a practice run of sorts, the laptop having a truly sucky keyboard as far as I'm concerned, flat and not with tiny legs like this one, though maybe I can plug this into that, who knows, and to be honest I have a lot of way bigger concerns and you might even say problems – say, um. no address to forward my mail to – than my being a technical dunce, so all I can say, and ask, is that you bear with me if there is a day or two when I do not keep my vow to post weekdays every day – since January 22nd now – back when I was a happily married, carefree kid.

Now I'm mostly just the carefree kid part. With potential computer issues. And Blog deficiencies. And, as that wonderful 80's band 'Missing Persons' once sang – "Destination Unknown." Like, five weeks from now. Wires in the right place or not.

A Blueridge

It's days like today I wish I'd started keeping a journal back from like when I was 10 up until yesterday. The ongoing scribbled story of my life. First, I think journaling is cool, and lately for me this Blog space has felt something what I expect writing in a journal feels like, especially since the third week in January when I announced a new post every day, Mondays through Fridays. The last month for sure. Plus, I think journaling is valuable as well as a clear record of people, places, things, times and dates, even what decade I'm trying to remember when something happened.

Like when I bought this Blueridge guitar. Was it the 80's? the 90's? the 2000's? I've been trying to puzzle this out this morning as I have recently rescued the Blueridge from where it has sat idly for years behind my mother's recliner up on the second floor where I will no longer be welcome soon. So the Blueridge has come down to the basement where I mostly live and write Morning Pages and this Blog and plan packing and storing and recycling and donating and throwing away behaviors, the 24-hour clock rushing around and forward and my time here rapidly coming to a close. Oh, I eat and sleep down here too, which barely matters. Anyway, the acoustic's down here with me these days and since it is within grabbing range every time I go to bed I have this last week been picking it up and slipping the strap over my neck and shoulder and muscle memory remembering chords and playing for five minutes until my non-calloused fingers start yelling at me to go to bed already.

There's a guy named Eddie Carlino in Medford, Massachusetts who followed his bliss and opened a guitar store a long time ago, which I just Googled and saw was

2003 – an aha for me re: the lost decade thing – since it was at Eddie's not long after he opened that I first heard about Blueridge acoustic guitars, which was a brand he carried and encouraged me to buy and which, as the photo proves, I did. But I did not buy one of the many Eddie had hanging on his wall. No, it was on one of my vacations to California and visiting/staying with my best friend Bob Zimmerman and me alone strolling down Telegraph Ave in Berkeley and coming upon a second-floor guitar shop in this open-air grouping of shops and I went in one afternoon and there was this used Blueridge, which I believe was on sale for $275 and, taking Eddie's advice because I liked and respected Eddie and hung around his store a bunch and even once bought a small cheap amp, I bought the Blueridge and walked back up Telegraph and over under the Sather Gate which is the entry from that direction onto the campus off UC Berkeley and went over and sat on a stone wall and began playing my new guitar – my first public performance ever, Yippee, and no one gave me money and no one told me to screw and pretty much no one paid me a lick of attention. But, still, how cool to first audition not 100 yards from where Mario Savio told the Berkeley kids and students to clog up the machine of big everything ('55 ?).

After a while, since I did then have calloused fingers and could play an hour or so, I walked the guitar back to Bob's in El Cerrito (I took the BART) and a few days later just before flying back to Massachusetts I brought the guitar back to Blue Note Music on Telegraph and had them ship it to me in Medford – which they safely did.

This morning the Blueridge has served as my journal, accurately reminding me of times in my life, and it's down here in the basement with me because this is simply another time in my life – more selling than buying – and in fact I pretty much am journaling the fading of my marriage and my kid being safely tucked away in a new and loving home and me soon enough going to hit the highway (once again) and all I'm bringing with me will be what fits in the Camry. And I may have sold all the electrics and amps, but the Blueridge is here in the basement, the strings breathing life, just a little, again. And there will be a place in my car for it, out there somewhere on the 5.

Hopefully I'll journal that journey too.

Which Side

I felt I had a long, organized, well-thought-out, word piece for this Couch Surfing home for today, this Wednesday, exactly six weeks since my life flipped over and the world changed in an instant – my world anyways, and my kid's.

So this morning up in the recliner, say 5:45, I had this cool idea forming about today's Blog, which would surely be a report of my internal weather which is the day-to-day goal, and then Wednesday happened and some very wonderful things happened including a degree of ongoing kindness toward and for me which continues to blow my mind, and is both affirming to me as a human and for me regarding humans. And I made another delivery to the independent bookstore, giving my life's books to such a deserving place, and deposited a bit of money in the credit union from selling microphones and a painting, and then I came home and tried making calls out in the backyard of a way less pleasant, and frankly for me, discouraging reality, but none of them went anywhere, and dinner is early tonight and I have three calls I care about, one of those more business-y things, from 5:30 on, and my point is the great Blog idea of many hours ago is gone – flown away. And I am tired and drained and all you get from me today is this speedy nothingness.

The Blog, which will use an extended version of this one's title when I write it – I'm hoping tomorrow – works from the questions of "Which side are you on?" Some of you may know that question, in its musical configuration. This won't be that.

Wrung-out Wednesday.

Which Side Are You On

On April 14th, a Wednesday, at almost exactly 11 o'clock in the morning my wife – beginning the talk she said she wanted to have, said to me, "This is going to be hard, especially for you, but I want a divorce." Yeah, it was hard, harder than almost anything, and it still is.

That afternoon I went for a long walk in the rare spring sun of Portland, a little under two and a half miles, and maybe halfway through called my best friend in Oakland, CA and I talked and cried and he listened and gave gentle advice and by the end of the walk, close back to "my house", I had committed to stay on my side of the street going forward – no matter what – and be on the best high alert I could muster every five minutes for my Higher Power's will for me. Now what? This was my new thing – "What is the will for me – the next five minutes – my side of the street?"

I am glad and also proud to say, in all honesty, I have done just that, forgetting the every five-minute thing for periods of a few hours here and there, but remaining on my side of the street. I have not been mean, I have not said mean things, I've tried my best not to be any kind of an asshole these final few weeks of living together. I've removed myself almost entirely to down into the basement. I haven't passed a lot of judgments and any that have come to me I've kept to myself. My goal has been to take care of my son Spenser and then take care of me and how that has happened has been through physical, emotional, and spiritual efforts nearly (but not) beyond my capacity as a 72-year-old long-time screw-up with a pretty gentle, hopeful heart for the world. Along the way, as friends and even new acquaintances have learned of my "situation" (the wife called it) I have been treated with amazing kindness and generosity and love.

Also, along the way, and increasingly with the passage of time, I have been advised in strong and then stronger terms to take better care of myself in a legal sense, to invoke my right for fairness after 10 and a half years of marriage, 11 years living together. And almost entirely I have accepted these caring bits of advice from nearly a dozen people now, and then let them go. It didn't fit with my vow, back around the 15th of April, to leave with grace and dignity. People have literally howled at me that taking care of myself and remaining with grace and dignity are not in battle with each other. They can co-exist. Still, I've felt good about my way of leaving – my son more and more secure – and been thrilled with a mostly smiling Universe.

Yesterday, a Wednesday late in April, and triggered by what felt like a petty meanness directed at me the night before, I walked out into the middle of the street. I made some phone calls and listened more carefully to the stick-up-for- yourself-better advice, and I could feel the quality of my, well, existence, change. I felt different. When I sat for my meditation this morning, in which I'm generally pretty quiet and often count from one to 10 over and over, slowly, my breathes becoming deeper and longer, this morning I could never get past "One", try as I would over and over, I couldn't get past the first "one". My head was swirling with likely or potential or possible courtroom language and recriminations and anger and all that shit I vowed the first day to leave alone. Honestly, call me naive, I'd never even thought about it until someone said it loudly to me. Anyway, I went to the recliner and drank coffees and opened my mind to the will for me, five minutes would be good, and, yeah – back over there where I belong.

By the time I got down here to write my Morning Pages, some five and a half hours ago now, I'd moved back over to my side of the street. I like it there. I have felt soothed and cared for there. I haven't felt afraid and don't feel afraid. I've actually discovered wonder and opening doors and windows – even some magic. My friendship with my best friend has been electrified, in a wonderful way, and people have come from my past to become part of my new present. To be honest, right here and now, I do have one remaining plan for a little "theater", what we long-time Yippies always called "Guerilla Theater", in the other take-care-of-myself way. I'll play with it this afternoon and I suppose it may roll into tomorrow's morning, but I'll keep a light heart, and all the while part of me will be thinking about what needs to get packed next and how best to keep looking for a new address and how lucky I am to have the friends I do.

At noon, on this Thursday – this is the side of the street I'm on. And I'm sticking to it.

Tra-la-la

Oh, late Friday afternoon, is it me or are the minutes, hours, and days whizzing by. Like it was just Tuesday when I was dropping Spenser at his soon-to-be new home over with Aaron in the next town of Gresham, 15 miles in driving distance but a route from one of Dante's lower levels of hell with lights and lights and more lights and your average Oregon driver, and – enough of that judging – anyway, here it is Friday afternoon and those three nights have come and gone quickly and how much did I really accomplish in terms of packing and completely redirecting my life those two days he was not here to need constant explaining to and comforting of. Hope it's more than it feels looking at all the odds and ends seemingly everywhere on a walk through this house I've lived in 11 years now – pretty much a record for me with the exception of the house I grew up in on High Street in Wareham, Massachusetts.

And Spenser gets it and then he doesn't and he looks forward – all the way back and after a stop for him at Subway – to sit in the living-room with his still step-mom and watch High School Musical 2, which even if I wasn't a basement dweller I'd slink down to the below-ground depths and watch Goliath or Bosch or something else cheery. But here I am, down here, a Blog to write and feeling a smidge Hunter Thompson-esque, the mojo machine in the corner screaming for copy, and me with traffic reports and the mental and spiritual twirlings of a kid with Down syndrome and his dad with who-knows-what. Charm, perhaps? Delusion? Maybe just sharing a little joke with the world.

Which is it for late Friday afternoon from down here in a Portland basement, my next-to-last Friday in this home which has been real good to me all this time – offered up some magic along the way. And ditto for the still wife. She's been real good for me. Even counting the last six weeks.

I could dial up YouTube and play Warren Zevon's "Accidently Like a Martyr" and get all morose. But that's not me. I think I'll find some elementary school choir, hopefully with kids from all races, singing something with "Tra-la-la" in it.

The Mysterians

These are the final five days in this house for me. This house into which I moved in May of 2010. The house in which I became an artist again after quite a long gap from the fourth grade. The house in which I wrote and published eight books, in the process becoming a poet and giving readings at the local – and my long-time fave – coffee house. Where I have cut the grass and watered the flowers, planted vegetables in less than optimum conditions with okay results. Where I daily rejoiced with my soulmate.

I have to leave Sunday. A young couple with a truck – her I've met (we almost created a Podcast together), him never – are coming early Sunday afternoon to try and haul my big bed up the small stairway from the cellar and a couple of beat but wildly loved recliners, a bookcase and a couple of small tables – all the things you'd expect a young boy to have gathered after seventy plus years. I've already hauled and dragged and prayed heavy boxes of books and Spenser's zillion t-shirts and DVD's over to storage, and the Sunday move is likely to take two trips and the young couple have said they will not accept money – my book

"Get in the Car" will suffice, throw a few greeting cards in for good measure. Kindnesses again.

We'll haul the few pieces to a garage I was gifted in exchange for a few of my paintings and then later in the day – Sunday – I'll make my way over to a spare room I've also been gifted for two of my paintings (my fourth-grade art teacher would be proud) and try to feel my way around in someone else's house for three weeks, you know that tip-toe be sure not to be rocking any boats, being a guest an all. You couch surfer. You gypsy.

It's supposed to be 96 in Portland by later afternoon today and I walked the first of my two, two-plus-mile walks at just after six this morning, beat the heat, escape domestic reality for a bit, me and runners and cyclists and a few fellow walkers. And birds – lots of birds. The second walk of the day will come after eggs and bacon and green beans – a replica of last night's meal (us Keto-ites eat a lot of the same meals) – and that walk will be out in, like Springsteen sang, the ninety-degree heat. (When Kitty came back to town.)

Next Monday, a week from yesterday, I'll come back to this house, key-less and hoping someone answers the door and decides to let me in, to pick up Spenser and grab the last of his stuff and his TV and DVD player and jam things in the car and drive him 15 miles and through too many lights and stop signs up to his new house – with younger, cooler, hipper caretakers. But no more Dad. I will be driving up many times through this new month, June, to visit my kid and encourage him to settle in and call his new home home. Come July we'll make do with airplanes and Zoom and phone calls.

I just did change of addresses at the post office for both of us. Spenser's was in fact where he's changing to. For me, well, I've borrowed to a friend's mailbox for a while, far away, because I was pretty sure they weren't forwarding all the junk and occasional important piece to a question mark.

You know how that song goes – 96 Tears.

Late

Late to the party, ho-hay, I made a thing with myself (vow seems too heavy, commitment too math-like), anyway I told myself I would write my first post from the laptop today – what with the imminent dissembling of the computer, day after tomorrow or next, and I better make sure I can get it done over there on the other side of the table and now it's past 8:30 tonight and the laptop has been silent since 11 hours ago when I concluded a zoom thing at Encinitas, California. And the day has drained and there have been highs, some glory I believe, the glimmer in the kindness of friendship and the rushing out the door to take in the sweet, early, early morning air. And there have been downs, not so much lows as the visual reminders that much remains to be done in leaving and the clock has little in the way of pity, it's more a consoling thing….

And if this sounds loose and scattered and you wish you were doing something else, then God bless ya, it's all good even the very hard stuff, and adventure seems to come through any old door when least expected and it doesn't ask much beyond my full attention. Which I'm pretty good giving these days.

So Wednesday's nearly gone and the first laptop Couch Surfer post need wait for another day and I think I might scout out some real early Jefferson Airplane and ease myself into dreamland.

Emotional Recuse

I sit here at my computer, late Thursday morning, and I could and maybe want to write many things here at Couch Surfing that – even me hearing them as I consider the words – would sound like feeling sorry for myself. I don't want to do that because that's not how I feel. I do not feel sorry for myself. My head hurts and my body hurts and my life is for sure akimbo, and just as surely my soul and child-like mind has been filled with wonder and blessing and possibilities I could never have imagined. And folks have come from the deep woodwork of my life and they have said – individually, collectively – we love you Bro, and we've got you and you've been working on the accepting help thing so let us help. And I have and I've been just filled up with gratitude. Really filled up. Fucking crazy amazing.

But, as I said a few sentences back, well, I was thinking it while I wrote what I wrote and I was thinking it more clearly on a very early morning walk six hours ago, and it's that with all the feelings I've been feeling these last now seven plus weeks – since the wife said I no longer want you, or want you here – over the last five or six days the energy of those feelings has waned. Clearly any feelings of tiny fear or broken-heartedness, of being blown away by the abundance of kindness, of having to bite my tongue when words – words without graciousness and so, without worth – bubble to my lips. All these feelings have been turned down, from high to simmer – good, bad, the physical discombobulations. Turned down.

I began noticing it a couple of days back, not so much auto pilot because I'd be truly screwed – as would my son Spenser – if I was coasting. The clock rushes along and the days dwindle and I'll be out of here before you can say next week, Spenser on my heels. No — now and all these weeks my keto-brain has been firing on nearly all cylinders and the daily long "To Do" lists get attention and devotion and necessary act gets crossed off one by one. So, it's not I've been checked out. I think it may be more a case of being used up – not all the way, like I just said, there are real needs which need all of me. No, it's the feelings part, which were electric and remarkable and wicked and super-charged from April 14 and right through to a few days back. And then I noticed I wasn't feeling so much anymore. Not so much of anything.

I don't think this is bad, it doesn't feel foreboding or, really, even concerning. It just is what it is. Maybe it'll be way different come next Tuesday and Wednesday and a week from today. Probably absolutely for sure come the first of July. Just here now, this morning, I'm not feeling a whole lot.

And, by the way, if there's a bit of a "Stones" quality to the title of this post, almost a misspelling, they're not my thing. Never have been. Except "Memory Motel". Yeah, that's a truly good one. I think I'll play it now. See what comes up.

Signing Off

Hello. This will be my lost post in the Couch Surfing Blog I submit from Portland, OR. I'm leaving Sunday. It feels like it's been a real good run, being here in Portland, on my own (mostly) for the first year and then luckily going on a 'Match' blind date and meeting a woman who became the love of my life, and my soulmate. In the last 11 years here I've become an artist, I've published two vastly different Blogs over a number of years, and I have self-published eight books – four of poetry (a big go figure) and three fictions and a non-fiction. More on that last one in a minute. This has all been under the umbrella of the wife's acceptance of my setting out on different paths and sort of morphing into the person I am today. Sort of like a scholarship.

Then seven weeks ago Susan said "No more" and here it is a Friday morning and there's something like 48 hours remaining in this house which has been my vibrant home, and then back the next day to pack off the kid for his new life – one for which he is excited, and stimulated in good ways, and likely on occasion he'll miss his old man pretty good too.

Sunday I move into a room I bartered for with art in the next town over – Milwaukie – for the rest of the month. The younger woman offering me this kindness of shelter is for sure a katrillion times hipper with electronics and the internet age, meaning I'm hoping with her help (mostly her) to have my soon to be disassembled computer re-assembled and me back here offering up these daily "weather reports" which pretty much flow out of my soul, via my two index fingers.

Sometime the very end of June, no later than the first day of July, I will say a final thanks to my very temporary roommate and head off to – honest, I ain't kidding – parts unknown. I do know the direction in which I'll point the Toyota Camry – and assuming I am back here early next week, which may be Tuesday what with the son's Monday move over to another surrounding town – Gresham – I will begin talking clearly and honestly – and, it being me – rather goofily about what I believe to be in store for me next. The geography of my "next". My one book of non-fiction, noted above, is titled "Get in the Car". Maybe you've read or perused through it. Its overall theme – spelled out and implicit – is to just go and get in the car. Go someplace. Make something happen. Be bold and expect, rightly so, mighty forces to come to your aid. It's part metaphor, the "get in the car" thing, and more actual.

And it is what I will be doing soon enough, traveling on a new path I didn't and never would have asked for but now see as chance to live a different life. Maybe one pretty cool. Another chapter. Friends have helped to get me there, to get me ready for the car. And the blue, blue highway. Helped more than I can say. I say Thank you.

But this post right here is the last one from right here. It is heart-breaking. And it's a new window as well. One to crawl through. Some new highway miles too.

A New Dawn

Grace Slick said that at Woodstock, with the Airplane. "It's a new dawn." Right before she said her kind of famous "Good morning people." I myself wasn't at Woodstock, kind of blew it skipping that, but my younger sister went. I know what Grace said, though, because I've seen the movie a bunch and listened to the soundtrack even more.

Anyway, the "new dawn" idea is most relevant for me today, waking up as I did in a new town, in a "guest" room, more angels at work in my life, like the young couple who moved my meager collection of furniture to the storage yesterday, the storage a garage gifted to me by yet another angel, bartered for a few pieces of art (like the room). So here I am, maybe four miles from where I've been the past 11 plus years, and in a couple of hours I'll head back to that place I called home so long to gather up my son and lots of his remaining things and hope they all fit in the car, which as I write this in a patio sun room is (my car) jammed already with the stuff of my life I'll bring along to the next place and space – and, yes, grace – in my life. Which I will talk about tomorrow.

Get the kid, move him into his new home, hit the Trader Joe's I love on the way back for some frozen meatballs and a couple of yellow bell peppers, return here (and I have a temporary key) and quietly – my hostess works long hours from home and will be just right over there from the stove and microwave – make something to eat and settle in. She did get my computer up and running last night – how this post is here – and besides all that wonder and continued generosity, I for the next three weeks have a cat as a roommate too. So cool.

Beginning the more of what just might be the next remarkable and amazing chapter of this life I still have this morning – I'm still here. Yesterday was hard, lots of sadness. Today there'll be some of that too. I'm hoping for a slice of easy does it tomorrow, when I will schedule nothing for the first time in a long time.

Good morning, people.

Just After Six

It's just after six Tuesday night. Somehow the plans to write an early afternoon post got scuttled. Actually, I'm sure I could relate in detail pretty much exactly how that happened – Bad phone call with perspective roommate – a big "No." Lost touch with angel offering two weeks from which to reconnoiter locally (not Oregon) for a new place, no one taking me serious about a rented room from 1000 miles away. He simply vanished. Longer walk than usual exhaustion. Noon Zoom from downtown somewhere. Wondrous phone call with a favorite old high school classmate, about a zillion years since last talk. Lots in common, some bad, lots good (mostly attitude and viewpoints of what's important, what with the numbers on our birth certificates.) Second crazily long walk during long tele call with long-ago college (Salem) roommate, updates and chuckles and dizzying whirls around a lopsided Milwaukie track.

Oh, did I mention the potential job interview, like, yikes, the kid going back to work at this stage of the game!

Somehow, every one of these actions, activities, day-dreamings, updates, calls happening and calls unanswered – somehow they are directly tied together. Kind of a go figure.

What I meant to write about, and I decided this yesterday after moving Spenser to his new home – and hearing he and his new clan were gonna be off to Idaho this morning – I decided I was going to share what's been going on in my mind and no doubt my soul about the always fun question of "Now what?" Then all this stuff happened and the minute hand giggled its speedy way around the dial and here it is 6:27 and this is the best I've got.

I promise tomorrow I'll spill the beans. Pinto or refried.

At least I hope I do. Keep that promise.

the faith

I had a vision yesterday of how this particular post would look, sound, and read. But that's all gone. The idea of living life one day at a time had never been more vivid and tangible for me, ever, 72 years worth and (thankfully) still counting. So, I (thank you Great Spirit) wake up today and the big eraser in the sky wipes clean the blackboard of my mind and now it's quarter past 11, late morning and I'm nearly seven hours into this day and I come here with as much anticipation as any other reader of what's coming next. News at 11.

A week, give a day or two, after the word "Divorce" hung in the air between my wife and myself, on a morning like so many since, too numbed to actually read a book, sitting with two cups of coffee in the old, beat-up pink recliner, meditation (call it) over, three steno pads and one larger notebook on the coffee table before me, I felt something like a presence – I cannot think of a better description – come into the living room. I didn't hear a voice, I didn't have a vision. It was just an idea into my head, and I know, into my soul as well. It was this – go to San Diego.

A smidge of relevant background is my wife (papers may be signed, I don't know, maybe ex-wife) grew up in San Diego, about 12 miles east from downtown, and I began with her visiting her parents beginning in 2010 – once or twice a year, I think maybe three times one year. Down to San Diego every year. And her parents had an old Corolla in great shape and their daughter was allowed its use, and I got to see and experience and really know San Diego. The beach at Ocean Beach, the pier at OB, the Saturday farmers market downtown in Little Italy, into and out of Lindbergh Airport a zillion times, Balboa Park, the art museum, seaport village. I went three times to Petco Park, the first time by myself, the next two with the father-in-law. We drove up the coast to Encinitas twice. Up the coast to La Jolla, to Pacific Beach, out to the tip of Point Loma. Walked the neighborhoods of Golden Hill and South Park, had coffee all over the city. I fell in love with the place. And it wasn't raining.

Begging would be an accurate description of my pleadings with the wife to please, pretty please, can we move there, over the last five years. Nope, not a chance. And then there was this word "Divorce" shimmering in the air and then I was in the recliner with coffee and a presence announced itself with go to San Diego. And as it dawned on me that come June 30 (after a month at a bartered-with-art spare room with a friend) I was going to be an old white guy without an address. Which was, even for gypsy me, scary but also, for sure, a window being thrown open. Crawl through here, Brah. Follow this path, Bro. Get in the car, kid. And it may have been that day or the next day or a couple of days later, whatever day it was, that's what I decided to do – go to San Diego.

First it was getting my son Spenser safe and sound – and loved – and I have done that with the help of angels and he's already vacationing in Idaho, likely trying to remember some old guy named Pops. And beyond taking care of Spenser, and the truly physically and emotionally and psychically being beaten up with the move and the moving out and away for good, I've summoned nearly all the strength of attention I've gathered these last 72 years and aimed it down the 5 to San Diego, and I've posted a hundred Craigslist posts looking for rooms and I've applied for part-time jobs to help with wicked high costs and I attended maybe a thousand Zoom meetings I tend to attend and made connections and put it out there and asked for help, and here it is three weeks before there is no address and nothing much is doing, sort of, and I'm doing what they all told me to do in the 60's and "Keeping the faith, Baby" and the adventure already – just in the searching – has been magical and mystical and attracted nearly indescribable generosity and kindness.

Those don't-drink-just-one-day people have a saying which is, "the Joy is in the Journey".

Ain't it the truth.

scammers get back

Today has been a day of irrationalities.

It began well, up on time, crack 'o dawn, all morning rituals, Morning Pages completed in the notebook resting on a hardcover Pablo Picasso Retrospective, which I carry around to open and be artistically stimulated but these days only serves as a desktop on the futon in Kate's sun-room which I lean over to write, and, oh, my back cries Mary.

I did that stuff and then I zoomed some cats and kitties in Encinitas, up the CA coast 25 miles from San Diego, and then I electrically trimmed my beard in Kate's backyard without a mirror to be all kinds of presentable and then – bam – had a zoom job interview – What? The kid heading back to the salt mines at 72? What? So, I had the interview, slightly coincidentally also in Encinitas, and my sense after the interviewer "ended the session" rather speedily was that the old Budster human service magic may have waned in 10 years of retirement. I've been wrong about self-assessment of how interviews have gone before, though, so I'm pledging (to me) to keep an open mind.

Here's where the truly irrational giggles its way onto the scene. After having thought I could maybe scrounge up a chunk of employment income to offset the wickedly stupid and for sure offensive high costs of living anywhere these days, and especially where I would and do want to live – San Diego, Oakland CA a close second – and then with the sense of, well, there goes that plan, I trundled over to the computer which Kate hooked up and got running for me on a low coffee table here on Kate's patio, so more leaning over and – Yow, my back! – I immediately went to the San Diego version of Craigslist and proceeded to reply to four or five very expensive listings and tried to convince their authors that it was me, the Oregon kid, marriage-less, homeless, and still filled with a giddy hopefulness – that would be their perfect roommate and, come on, what do ya say? Every one of these posts with the exception of one asked for a rent sum beyond my monthly Soc. Sec. payback from the feds. And having said that – and already back there in the first sentence outed myself as wicked irrational – before you run to the reply space and ask me just what the "f" I'm doing, I want you to know that being worried about being considered truly stupid is so far down my list of things of concern these days it barely registers under an electron microscope. In other words – don't bother.

Plus, I've been sending out replies to folks listing rooms for rent for six weeks now and have received none in return. In my mind's eye I see someone looking twice at their screen to make sure what they are seeing is real – some old white guy, think Walter Brennan, wants to move in and be roommates – after the laughing dies away – hahahahaha-hahahaha……. they hit delete. "Fucking loser" I imagine them saying which, that, makes me chuckle a little.

Instead, you know who gets back? Scammers. Scammers get back. Every single time. Can't let shit fo' brains get away. Fortunately, after traveling only once far down the road of compliance, stopping only with the first and last in the mail please thing, I've learned to spot early on those who live for and by scamming. An early tip-off is they can't and/or don't bother to spell for crap – "Lovely Rume for Rental. Free Tilities Two. Won't Last. Replie with Socal Security." See, I done honed my detection skills.

The fact remains, though, apart from scammer proclivities, that I have behaved irrationally a bunch already, and it's still early. And, with three weeks exactly left before no more address anywhere, I'm feeling kind of spirited today. A bit mischievous. Like I'm right where I'm supposed to be.

I'm in love Friday

Kind of a Cure anagram there, if you can dig that.

And coming is stream of consciousness, no available topic, updates to friends including a call from my bosom pal Garden State Mike from over there by the Jersey shore, lost track of time and logged on wicked late to the second Zoom meeting of the day, down in San Diego where I have promised myself my biggest bestest ever presence through the weekend, so one in Encinitas early and one downtown noon and likely number three right by the Pacific over in Ocean Beach later – we locals like to call it OB – and see that last line was what those don't-take-the-first-drink-which-is-the-only-one-which-can-get-you-drunk folks call "Acting as if", see, maybe if I act like a local I'll become one, and to be clear I will invoke voodoo and witchcraft and hoodoo and each and every mystical practice I can conjure up in this righteous pursuit of an SD life, and I don't know how it's going to work out, honestly, and I've said Oakland CA – a long lost lived-before love of mine – is door number two and I did have an actual non-scammer reply from a guy there yesterday and we went back and forth with emails, visuals and neighborhoods and cool stuff like being able to walk to what's probably my second favorite Trader Joe's on the planet from his house and it was left I supplied my tele number and please call so we can talk (kind of) in person, any time after 10 Friday and here it is 1:30 and no Oakland dude call, and while I do not feel like I can't go on nor do I feel as though all of my hope is gone I am sure hoping he'll reach out – cause I'll be there.

Which is a fun, second musical reference to this finger-tapping twist like I did 55 summers ago and with the second round of double coffees in process and within my milieu, here on Kate's patio on a rainy Oregon day and the forecast is for four more coming, and I have a plan to go to the storage garage and take a couple of hours tomorrow afternoon and bundle up every box tight and properly labeled for shipping down to SD (there's that "act as if" again) and a stop sometime this weekend to resupply my meager stash of food from my absolute number one favorite Trader Joe's in Portland, and I get this is your weekend and why bother taking time to read this ramble and I got no good answer for you, but thanks for showing up again, I'm thrilled and wildly grateful every time someone else tells me they're keeping up with the kid's comings and (hopefully) down-the-coast goings.

So, if you are out there this Friday afternoon – my thanks.

Loop de Loop

I sat down here, Monday 1:20, leaning over a small ottoman on which sits my laptop. On which I'm typing this – amazingly slowly – my first ever Blog from here, and what I remember as a kid's song – "Here we go loop de loop" came floating on into my head, I guess the strangeness of setting and the sense of I better be learning to use this machine a heck of a lot more than just the now-beyond-regular zoom meetings (the Dell here with a camera, the desktop Lenovo over there on Kate's coffee table with none. – Mr. high-tech, that's me.)

And the coffee maker's out here as well so the perking doesn't wake Kate back in the house from her 5:30 slumber after my crazy-early meditations and there's a transitory carry-it-all-along feel to my life now and I suspect for some time to come. And this weekend had crazy emotional and psychic ups and downs, yesterday itself themed by the Ohio Players "Roller Coaster of Love", and I find myself stopping and it could be on the couch or in the meditation chair or on this ottoman companion, or way over on the lop-sided track in the park a quarter mile away, my third or fourth time around, yup I stop and realize a distinct thought has entered my life space – kind of like the loop de loop thing but usually bigger in terms of life enhancing and impacting choices – and I pay attention to the arrival and take note and so often in the last two months – today the exact anniversary of April 14 and the divorce talk – I make a decision and take action. Some of yesterday's decisions brought me up and some took me down and I was so weary ending the day, and I'd learned Spenser was staying in Idaho an extra day meaning today was mine to easy does it, please, and yet early on new and important thoughts showed up and I just went and acted on them. Like I've been doing since the middle of April. And the fact is there's 17 more days in this bartered living space to see how they turn out.

All of which explains – to me at least – the little kids singing loop de loop, I swear I can hear their very voices from more than 60 years back, and one choice effects another and that was that and okay this is this and well that's settled, for better or worse, and now what? And if this is more mush thanks for staying if you have and good choice if you bailed because this Monday I have a sharp awareness of time and my oldie-car calendar is open over there on Kate's couch and it looks at me in a keep-me-in-mind-Holmes way, and I've zoomed this morning to a couple of beach towns in California and texted to Encinitas and been rejected or good lucked from all over, and yesterday I sent out updates to about 15 people who have been the most kind and generous and loving with and toward me these last eight weeks and I could write a new one today and it'd be real different and honest and truly all me, which is pretty much this Blog space as well, now kind of cool, sort of, and perhaps mystical in the fact I am couch surfing at 70 – with new decisions today and a new couch now needed the first half of next month.

And when all is said/done and I check for typos and possibly a word switcheroo or two for easier reading I'll hit the blue "Publish" button up there and among so many firsts here at age 72 will be another – Blogging off the laptop.

Oh my head

Here's the second dictionary definition of "labile" – "Of or characterized by emotions that are easily aroused or freely expressed, and that tend to alter quickly and spontaneously; emotionally unstable."

Someone's been reading my mail.

But first, let me take a stroll down memory lane all the way back to 1984, 1985, some of '86. I was working for a small outfit called the 'Drug and Alcohol Resource Program' based in Stoneham, Massachusetts, like eight miles north of Boston. We worked out of a reclaimed small tool factory, and while I was in the office a fair amount I was also assigned as an "in-school outreach counselor" for two schools a little north – Reading and North Reading High Schools. The powers that be gave me a room down a little-used corridor at Reading High School and I was grateful and have a few good and distinct memories from there. But it was way different at North Reading where the Principal, Dr. William Butler, welcomed me with open arms saying "We'll take any help we can get", and I was in and out of classrooms sharing my meager wisdom and hanging around corridors and actually began an official don't-drink-today (in the book and everything) meeting Friday mornings in the basement. But, the big deal was my own office in the guidance area, I mean me and whoever rolled in which were actually a bunch of different kids who I sat with for a couple of years and listened to rants and howls and goofy giggles, and looking back I was so blessed with that opportunity to be of some weird kind of help. And there were these two girls who always dropped in together and one of them told me she liked to walk down the middle of the road because she felt alive then, and that same girl would always say her favorite expression, which was this: "Oh my head."

And "Oh my head" meant oh my life and oh the craziness and hopelessness and my wild chances to shine and I love my friend and I hate everyone else and life's wicked hard and I walk down the middle of the road, and "Oh my head" was quiet and hallucinatory and all-inclusive, and without asking I decided to borrow it for some of those reasons and more of my own and – swear to God – I've been saying "Oh my head" out loud into the bright of day and the dark of night ever since. Let me say it right here, right now, because it fits.

"Oh my head."

Remarkable, and not surprising in the least, this isn't what I meant to blog about today. Nah. Go back to the first two paragraphs. Way earlier I was sitting in the Kate chair which has become a substitute for my morning recliner and I'd asked for help and guidance and – please – understanding of what's the will for me? – what's the plan? and I received two clear messages shortly thereafter and I realized I had changed my mind about where I wanted to live the rest of my life again, six times since last Saturday morning, three times alone on Sunday. Where I want, where I should, where I'm supposed to, what's the Great Spirit's plan, all of it. And the word "labile" came to mind and I googled the definition and it's up there in the first paragraph. That is exactly me these last two months, especially these last two weeks. Altering quickly……. emotionally unstable…….

And while typing the line "Someone's been reading my mail" the girls from NRHS came walking into the borrowed guidance office in my mind and one said "Oh my head" and it made and makes perfect sense, here now today, and the signs to me this morning – crystal clear – said you need to move here, Brah, get with the program, and I ate some brekkie and went for a second walk and mailed a copy of "Milky Dent" to an old high school classmate who never said the "Oh my head" thing but is one of that book's heroes, then I came back to Kate's patio and my email and an entirely different life direction said "Hello." (OMH). And as a postscript of sorts for anyone who likes to find their way through and out of mazes, the last person who donated fifty bucks to me in the "GoFundMe" account another high school classmate set up was a name I did not recognize but his note along with the contribution said I'd helped him out at Reading High School. And a couple of weeks before that a girl from North Reading High School – not one of the walk-down-the-middle-of-the-road girls – said she wanted to buy two of the paintings I'd pictured on Facebook for $25 each and then I found a PayPal payment for $1000 and a written explanation that I'd helped her more than I would ever know.

Which, again, doesn't have much to do with "labile" except being tangibly more of wild emotional experiences I've been experiencing these last eight weeks, and I don't know if it's what goes around comes around or simply more of the Universe grinning at me or karma or just there's really nice people looking for the chance to share their niceness. I do know, here today Tuesday the 15th, I don't have a definitive answer where to live and no address at all July 1 and for sure a crazy fucking amazing life right now and labile is the kid's calling card today.

And the best I've got – other than a wealth of unending gratitude for grown-up children – is I'm all ears.

I'm serious. I'm all ears.

Zip codes

Real early quickie today. The plan is to head up to Gresham and visit with Spenser. He returned later last night from a week in Idaho with the new family and in-laws – all of whom he adores. Therefore, it was not a surprise when he indicated little to no interest hanging out with Dad today – or going forward. In fact, I was thrilled to hear it. His life's been majorly uprooted and now he gets this wildly different life with younger and (probably) cooler people and his degree of being psychically stimulated likely rises and that's all good, even if there's some of me feeling sad about seeing him less before rarely seeing him at all.

We got closer as companions during Covid, and a lot more so the last couple of months as imminent fugitives from a life we'd known a long time and on to another – in his case, with people he knows and loves (in his Spenser way); in mine, on a new path, what so far has been an amazing adventure filled with glowing generosity and kindnesses, funky and fun invitations, and the slightly scary and even more thrilling reality that "the plan" for me has yet to be revealed. If there's a zip code out there with my name on it, I can't tell you today what it'll be.

Maybe I'll swing the cursor back up to the now-empty "Add title" line and type in "zip codes". I think that feels right. Spenser's got a new one, which may change soon, the lease is up, to another town or possibly another state. Mine for sure is changing to another town and another state – and if the creek don't rise and there ain't no meltdown – it will be a state with a heck of a lot more sunshine that the one I've been living a wondrous life in the last 12 years.

So, in an hour I'll drive 15 miles to visit my son and hopefully he's awake and wants to hang with his pops and I'll lower the number of times to visit from there, and possibly even head out toward somewhere south and way closer to the Pacific sooner than planned and like I said to Kate earlier this morning – my life feels really interesting to me these days, and I'm trying to pay it my best attention.

Here's a fun long-ago picture of Spenser, who is a real cool dude.

consequential conspirators with mi vida loca

It's 12:33. I innocently began completing the job application for the job I may – it's possible – I could have one of these not-too-far-in-the-future days in a sunny southern California beach-side town. I figured it would take 20 minutes – 30 tops. I began at 10:18. You remember that song by The Who – "Out of my brain on the 5:15″? I get that the numbers are not exact – 10:18, 12:33, 5:15. But, trust me, the gist of the song and later a significant scene in the movie 'Quadrophenia" is that the main dude was losing it, maybe it had long been lost and clarity was only then arriving. I don't know. But after literally cursing and howling and weeping, gnashing teeth and yanking employment memories from the farthest reaches of my mind, for two hours all I could think of was one of my son

Spenser's most recent and oft-repeated sayings – "That damn divorce."

First, on April 14th, there was the pain of my partner saying she wanted a divorce – the deepest pain I've ever felt. It's cold, bright starkness has diminished over time, the passing eight weeks. But the pain lingers. There was also the physical beating on my already beaten-up and seven-decade used-up body, packing and moving all the stuff. The mild trauma of recycling and donating and selling for pennies on the dollar much of the most important "stuff" of my life. The worry for and about Spenser – his hearing it, his dealing with it, his ability to move on.

****

All what you'd call life "heavy" stuff. But those two paragraphs above were scribbled 90 minutes ago because right after typing "his ability to move on" came a phone call from a guy in Oakland who had the best, most affordable, great location room in the city and I'd delayed chasing it down because of San Diego glitterings, and last week he told me he'd rented it to some UC Berkeley grad, except here he is on the phone to me today and the grad's credit is funky – which should have tipped me off – and the call went on and on with me being grilled about ability to pay and proof of soc security and proof of savings and he didn't seem all that moved about me saying a primary reason for me to be excited about Oakland and a new life there (beyond proximity to Gavin and David) was the racial make-up of the city, like my old hometown in Massachusetts and completely unlike all-white Portland (and even Encinitas for that matter, though they do have that body of water right there). The point being I became way ready to hang up from that unpleasant call which followed the hideous job app which that, filling it out, followed waking to an email from a way expensive but the absolute best room availability I gushed over two weeks ago and heard back nothing, where I'd most want to be in San Diego – "Are you still interested in the room?" – and I flipped with joy and wrote back my biggest yes and I was sent a bunch of questions and answered them promptly, thoroughly, and joyfully except the one when could I look at the room because I can't from up here, and now six hours have passed and no further word.

Proving, to me anyway, that what I began to write about and intended to write about – that beyond all the truly terrible big stuff has come all this hangering-on other stuff which is crazy making and up-and-down roller-coaster stressful – that's real. And yet sometimes I write these daily weather reports, the insides of me and my soul, and I hear myself two-finger typing the words and it sounds like moaning or at least whimpering and oh, poor me, and I swear that's not it – that's never been it since my friend began calling me every day from day one forward and my life has been filled these couple of months with such gracious generosity and kindness…….and for sure magic.

And wonder. Big, big wonder. Think of it – so far today, and it's just three in the afternoon, I've had an email about maybe the greatest living space in the world from Golden Hill in San Diego, I've filled out a never-ending, wicked demanding job app from some company in Encinitas CA which, the job, would allow me to be of great service to the planet while hanging with surfer buds in a glorious SoCal beach town, and I've had a phone call from a fabulous neighborhood close by the Oakland Lake and my second-favorite Trader Joe's on the planet, all here on Kate's patio where I've been living and will keep on living through the end of the month for the price of a couple of paintings. I've made an appointment for next week at my credit union to be taught how to deposit pay checks from a thousand miles away. I've meditated on the patio and again out in the blessed sunshine, Oh, I had a 5am urge to text my long-lost Provincetown and fellow gypsy friend Keith just to say hello and he wrote back he's been following along with mi vida loca and texted me the name of a woman and her tele number because she could possibly have a room for me in Malibu. Yup, that Malibu.

So, I began noting feeling crazy ("Out of my brain on the train") with all the attendant requirements for moving my life forward after the reality of divorce, and then I review the day and, come on Buddy, will wonder ever cease? It's just dues, Bro (I hear the Universe whispering with a gentle smile), and I'm lucky to wake up another day and get to suit up and show up, even when it isn't always fun. Even when it's extra-strength hard.

Because my life is amazing today. How do you beat that?

Last time things

I went walking down the very steep hill from the East Moreland parking lot into Oaks Bottom today, this Friday. It's a sacred place for me and it's felt entirely sacred and generous in its natural abundance for all 10 or 11 of the last years I've been one of its visitors. I've probably averaged four or five times a season, June through September, after and before the rains. From up top, just at the edge of the tarred lot, you can see Mount St. Helens on a clear day. Today was clear. See:

The trail plunges down from the lot – and what goes down must trudge back up at journey's end – and out into this amazing meadow. Up a ramp from there onto the famous walkway which runs from downtown Portland and right down from the house in which I lived 11 years and out east into the County. You walk that maybe half a mile with lots of bikers and joggers and fellow walkers and sometimes blue herons in the water to the right, sometimes a dancing hummingbird, and, with life "opening up" again, the sound of kids howling and screaming and laughing with ever-loving delight from over on the left in the Oaks Amusement Park. After a while you cut to the right under railroad tracks and on tar a little more until there's a right into the woods and along the swampy, rush-filled, electric with red-winged blackbird glory that is Oaks Bottom. I've been blessed with up close looks while passing through one of those so many times with an owl eight feet away and raccoons and deer and ospreys and eagles swooping, a zillion ducks, and dragonflies glittering – all within the ever-present aural background music of bird song. Eventually, less than a quarter mile from back out into the meadow and the steep climb back to the car, there's a lookout place to the right. Today I stopped – longer than usual, which is usually long enough – and saw this:

I wasn't fortunate to see the flash from the red of their red-winged blackbird wings today, but the unmistakable conversations between dads, moms, and kids was everywhere. Oh, lucky me.

I took longer than usual on this walk today, stopping, staring, dawdling, hanging out with natures children, because I knew it was my last time there. My last time down into Oaks Bottom, my last time through the meadow I love, where so often hummingbirds have come to play with me – "He's back," I bet they say, and they join me for a while. My last time walking over the dirt and needle and stone path through those nothing really very special but still filled with wonder if you look for it woods. I looked today and I saw it today and while I was looking and while I was seeing, right there at the very front of my brain was the knowing – last time, Brah.

There have been many of those "last time" moments the past month. Some I was thinking this is probably my last time, even more I've spent my last time in or doing or with and it didn't even register. Until later. But mostly I know it. Most of the things I love will be over in another couple of weeks because the Universe has a plan for me and my Higher Power never stops caring for me, and right now I don't know or see the happily ever after part of it. But it's there.

And doing last time things, like walking Oaks Bottom today – and making memories along the way – is part of the deal.

Hooray for Luray

I was married in a large bed/breakfast kind of place on top of a mountain in Luray, Virginia. There was a woman (Zeta) who was legally certified to perform the ceremony by Page County and the state of Virginia. There was the woman filling in and running the 'Inn" that day. There was the bride and me. The four of us.

It wasn't hot that day like it is here today in Milwaukie, Oregon. Probably past 95 now. I've been in Kate's house – for the price of a couple of paintings and the no-price-on-it realm of friendship – for a little over two weeks now and have parked myself, other than sleeping in the spare bedroom, in her glassed-in patio room. I've loved it there and written the last 10 Couch Surfing inner-weather reports from the patio. Yesterday, in the 93 degree heat, the room became an autoclave. Truly wicked. I punked out mid-afternoon and came in here to my temporary sleeping place, where I am right now, for refuge. I'm here now because after a morning of some errands – tutorial at the credit union re: the art of depositing checks from 1000 miles away. A walk under the towering shade trees of Laurelhurst Park, which, thinking about it, maybe that was the last one of those. A stop at T-Mobile because no one could hear me when they called me or I called them – dx, loose memory chip. A run up to Fred Meyer to fill the gas tank and not have to do it early before making the evil light-infested drive up to Gresham to see Spenser early tomorrow. Oh, a stop at my favorite Trader Joe's on the planet, surely not the last time there, and dawdling a long time in the air conditioning, talking with a friend going through marriage troubles of his own, another guy on his way with his son to visit Mount Katahdin in Maine in a couple of weeks, a stop at Fenway Park for good measure, asking about becoming FB friends to stay connected, Sarah behind the manager's counter, telling each one I'd just been on the phone with Spenser who said to say hello because he's loved them all these years – and vice versa.

Anyway, I returned from the errands and the patio was a Dante Hell level and I came into the bedroom – which ain't no party temperature wise – and called Spenser's Personal Agent to update on the boy's new life, a few updates re: this boy's too. And I brought the laptop in here with me and it's resting on my right leg, which is crossed over my left, here on the bed, all windows closed and shades down darkness, and while I have seen for years people doing their computer thing with laptops resting on their laps, this right here right now is an absolute first for me. And when I press 'Publish" twice – very soon kids – I'll go back into the patio and look on the computer – the real one on the table – and see if it worked. And if it did, I'll twist and shout in celebration, mostly in my mind, too hot for all that activity.

The first paragraph here, yet another in my increasing visits down memory lane as memories of all my life rush more and more into my psyche, I think I thought of that day because after the wedding and the cake and goodbyes to Zeta and see you in a while to the housekeeper fill-in, the newlyweds spent their first afternoon as a betrothed couple in the sort-of-famous Luray caves. Google it, you'll see. And it was really cool down in those caves. Really cool. Just like I bet it is today on the sunny, marine'd-air southern California coast,

Which, that, may be another story.

Bushes and gypsies

I was just out trimming a number of bushes in Kate's yard – in preparation for a new windows operation early tomorrow – and helping some to earn my keep for days past and days remaining here in a sacred space of generosity in Milwaukie, Oregon.

I'll be off in an hour to make the drive to Gresham and spend the day with Spenser – days with Spenser numbered, decreasing in number quickly. Make the best of them, Bro, I tell myself. Be gentle and loving and affirming. Tell him

"You got this", exactly the way the Universe has been telling me you got this these nine weeks now.

I was out walking five laps on the lopsided track around the corner and down the street from Kate's house early, just after six, and on the first or second time around I realized that I had exhaled. I'd stopped with the kind of frantic, surely urgent, next right thing act after act which has been under my highest high beams for two months. And that all the crazy thoughts I've entertained and danced with and even sobbed with these last couple of days were me letting out my breath – breath its feels like I've held for what seems like forever. And it came to me I could see the plan for me – my plan – going forward. Clearly. And it came to me that I could go back – or even ahead – and fix stuff which may need fixing next week or next month or next Valentine's Day. What's permanent these days?

The first day, the very first day of my divorce, Gavin in Oakland pointed out the Fleetwood Mac song "Gypsy" to me – and how that (the song's title character) exactly was me that day and the days coming. And after a while, a day or two, I understood. And I for sure get it right here today, as laps have been strolled and bushes have been trimmed and my son's waiting and it's come to me the only business I have with the world today is to be here now.

Like 7 inches from the mid-day sun

I emailed and/or FB messaged 15 of the 18 people whose names I have on a list on a page in a steno pad with the title "Keep these folks updated always" (underlines included) – people who have reached out to me persistently and lovingly with kindness and generosity far beyond any expectations I may have had, if I'd had any in the first place, caring about and for me as word spilled out about my wife's request/demand for a divorce. I've expressed thanks and gratitude all along, every single day since the first day when I called Gavin in Oakland sobbing and he said I'd be okay and began holding me up with daily phone calls – "I've got you, Bro" – and others joined in, with shimmering support in all shapes and sizes. I began saying "thank you" almost all the time. My mother would be proud.

So eventually I created this list – woefully short when I think of everyone who could and ought to be on it, like Maria Flores in a Senior Services program in San Diego who emailed me day after day offering direct advice and referral information and ongoing encouragement. She's not on the list but she should be and I can't even think how long this list of names would bend and wind and linger and curve around corners if I got them all. Then, a couple weeks ago I thought I owed more than 50 "thank you's" a day so I gathered this list of particular angels and wrote a thorough "update" of where I was in the world that day – yes, where physically, but more psychically and emotionally and spiritually. And this morning I listened to the 4:35 alarm in Kate's spare room and came out and prayed for the right things and sat for 23 minutes and walked the lopsided track around the corner five times and wrote my morning pages and zoomed into one of those zoom-y meetings, this in Carlsbad on the California coast north of San Diego – just north of a town called Encinitas. And along the way I kept feeling inspired to add to today's "To Do" list and one action added was writing and getting out there the "where I'm at of me" today, and now 15 have received it and many have got back with feedback echoing what Dick M always said to me back there in '84 – "You're right where you're supposed to be."

The three names I have yet to add a check next to are my friend in Oakland, and we're talking tonight and since we talk daily knows all the "at" stuff already; an old high school classmate who I tracked down a couple of weeks ago after not talking with for decades and while talking I realized he was one of the main characters in "The Files of Milky Dent" and it made me happy he was in there and to remember it, and I mailed him a copy of "Milky" a couple of days later. I'll figure how to update him. The other guy I met in Provincetown, down the tip of Cape Cod, back in 2007, who I haven't seen once since but have had a remarkable ongoing telephone relationship with – electric – until he faded a little this past year. But he's on my list, just the other day he was trying to hook me up with a room in Malibu, CA.

I'll share the updates I sent/am sending to the 18 today here on Couch Surfing soon. I haven't felt the spark to do so channeling through me to this Blog space yet – though I have dropped the occasional hint. Anyway, thanks for reading. This feels less of my emotional writing self and more of my old "reporter" life. I think that's okay once in a while.

Carlos Santana fans will recognize the title of today's entry. The National Weather Bureau forecast for the Portland/ Milwaukie metro area the next five days goes like this – Thu – 86, Fri – 95, Sat – 107, Sun – 111, Mon – 107. (Followed by 96, 94, and 94 – taking me right up to a week from this Friday.) Like the song says – "It's a hot one."

I bet it's not so hot on the SoCal coast. And the title of another of my books is "Get in the Car".

Hmmm….

Finally, I got the invitation

Out early this morning, on the lop-sided track, I heard my Higher Power say to me, very clearly — "Welcome to the party."

Kitty's back

Today's Friday, and between you and me, this time exactly one week from now – it's 3:41 pm Friday June 25 – I'll be in some state of mesmerizement, gunning it south on the 5, having left the greater Portland metro one last time , driving since daylight and hopefully driving another hour or two to glide past the halfway point between here where I am right now and that place where my heart and soul and pretty darn sure the Great Spirit wants me to be — in the greater San Diego metro area.

My phone says it's 91 outside now, which maybe a lowball figure, and the next three day's forecasts are for, daily Saturday through Monday, 107, 114, 112. That'll be hotter than I've ever been and I've hunkered down here in Kate's house in Kate's spare room, having fled the glassed-in Bunsen burner patio, continuing to do what has inspired me as necessary and the next right thing, and so far today I've done all the usual morning stuff including a way-early-before-the-building-heat walk and zoomed folks in a North San Diego beach town, and more recently here in the spare room where I've so gratefully laid my head the last three weeks I have gotten myself recertified in CPR and First

Aid and only a few moments ago enrolled in the Kaiser network for Southern California – whose monthly "Senior Advantage" payments are less than Oregon's. Go figure.

The CPR re-cert was a must for a part-time job which may be waiting and the insurance is its own must for us older cats, and I guess sitting here with the laptop on the bed and me in a chair leaning forward and the low back muscles having a good laugh, the point of where my thoughts and index fingers have taken me (and you) since I sat down with not a thought in my head is that I've been blessed again today – almost countlessly – and again, like almost every day these last two months with the amazingly righteous help and encouragements from so many, I've hauled myself up, suited up and showed up, and gone on to the "Now whats?" of the day. And got shit done.

Lately song titles have figured in Blog post titles and I hope you know the one above, just a wonderful rock and roll song from Bruce Springsteen's second album, my favorite, "The Wild, the Innocent, and the E Street Shuffle." Here's one of the lines from "Kitty" – "And them tin cans are exploding out in the ninety-degree heat."

Heat's been on my mind, cannot avoid it, and music. Following my bliss and learning all over again how to let people help me in such generous ways. Way more connectedness with a power greater than myself too – let's call her Kitty today – and following the path opening in front of me.

Fridays, I guess, rambling along, and next week's ought to be pretty different.

Details Monday.

Encinitas

I just left Encinitas – electrically, on the computer winds of the internet. Zoom-traveler. It won't always be that way, the ethernet coming and goings. Forth to and back from Encinitas. It won't be that way next week.

I said to my fellow Encinitas Zoomers this morning that a very terrible thing had happened to me two and a half months ago. The unimaginable worst. But peeking out from behind that terrible thing was something shiny, something hopeful. Something remarkable and amazing. I've said this here to you. A week or so after the divorce conversation I was having real early coffee and something I've described – accurately – as a presence entered the wife's living room and very clearly encouraged me to go to San Diego. I've said this here to you as well – the wife's from San Diego and her parents remain there and we began from right away being together going down to visit and getting the second car and tooling all over greater-SD, swimming at Ocean Beach, lunching at Hodad's, wandering through the wonders of Balboa Park, the Saturday downtown farmer's market – all of it. I fell in love and I had no problem with begging and I begged to leave the Portland rain (sometimes it gets kind of hot here too) and move to SD and the wife would have none of it and then she was sending me away and a presence said, "Then you go. Go on now. Shoo." And I turned all the energy and devotion and attention and soulfulness asking for and accepting help I could gather, and, yet, with all that righteous energy there was never one offer allowing me to land in San Diego.

But there was in Encinitas. In fact, after seven weeks or so, all paths were leading to Encinitas. The only room ever offered to me up here from down there – in Encinitas; a possible/likely/almost for certain job waiting – in Encinitas. People offering me a spare room from which to look and scout – in Encinitas. And this too – I see you Ocean.

The presence I felt that morning the third week of April, I'm thinking now, wanted me to aim for San Diego and right there around San Diego would make it real as well, and Encinitas is 25 miles up the coast – in what's called San Diego's North County – a 30-minute drive to all the downtown SD places I love and have visualized myself hanging out in. It's 30 minutes to Golden Hill, to Ocean Beach. It's 30 minutes to Balboa Park, the farmer's market, the museum, the Padres and Petco. It's five minutes to the Pacific Ocean. The crazily expensive rent for the room promises to be offset by a very part-time job in which I'll get to work with and for and be supportive to a young man with Down syndrome, who, through phone conversations and a Zoom interview, sounds a whole lot like Spenser Cushman. And if that falls down and I cannot long afford the rent? There are people there – in Encinitas – who've promised shelter.

Remember how I've talked often about my first "mentor" of sorts – Dick M – and those encouraging words he so often had for me – "Your Higher Power didn't bring you this far to suffer." "You're Higher Power has a plan for you." "You're right where you're supposed to be."

This Friday morning I'll point my car south on the 5 and aim toward San Diego, and if the creek don't rise and there ain't no meltdown, slip off an exit 25 miles or so north of SD, late Saturday afternoon, and drive on in to this new life being presented to me in Encinitas.

This morning, here at Kate's dining room table, I'm pretty sure it's right where I'm supposed to be.

Tuesday blues and greys

- out early on the lop-sided track, beating the ongoing heat, I realized I was missing walking with my wife. My all-time favorite walking-with-human. They say we don't regret the past – I don't know.

- yesterday it reached 114, they predict 97 today, like some cold front's gone through, people looking forward to 97. Life's kind of relative at times.

- i'm doing things and thinking about doing things and planning to do things here around Kate's house which bear the flavor of leaving. As in here is coming a big, big ending.

- last night it was decided, between Gavin and me, I'd spend Friday night in Oakland, with him, two fabulous gifts and blessings….Gavin….Oakland. Who knows when I'll get there, I was just writing route directions and specifics, it's 10 hours or so, maybe only four turns between Kate's house and Gavin's house. I'll miss the early walk here, get going early and all that, I'm hoping me and Gavin can get a walk in down Telegraph or some other sacred street.

- also, amidst the world of maps and wicked far distances and likely being really tired by then I was googling whether it will be better to stay on the 5 straight through LA to Encinitas or swerve over toward the coast and get on the 405 on the westside and take it all the way to where it re-joins the 5, down in Irvine, where I crashed at the University back in the summer and fall of '82 with my high school pal Nicky and his wife in grad housing and couch-surfed a while and did pretty cool and fun things down in San Clemente, and if there are no big bumps and hiccups I'll be cruising through San Clemente sometime Saturday afternoon, continuing on into this unexpected and shimmering new door thrown open in my life.

- and talk about San Clemente, there's a guy who works at my favorite Trader Joe's in the world, in Portland, who's from San Clemente and he was always friendly and especially kind to my son Spenser, makes me like San Clemente more, and I spent a bunch of afternoons running on the high school track in San Clemente and nearly drowned at the beach there once after a shift at MacDonald's, but didn't, and I have already determined and decided and vowed to myself that once I'm settled into and just another everyday cat from Encinitas I'm going to jump on the 5 north some day and drive up to San Clemente, it's 34.7 miles, and do some of my old San Clemente things as a kind of honoring to and for this long bountiful quite often interesting life I've been given so far.
- today's a Spenser day, my last time with him for two-three months, and he was throwing up from the heat last night, I learned late, and I'm sure hoping he's back to his usual cool self today. I'm aiming for my best dad self.
- my gratitude level for everyone who has helped me arrive at this very spot this very today morning is high. It's real high.

- i'm saying "thanks" a lot – and digging it.

It wasn't my idea, Noreen

All of this, everything since the ides of April, all the everything of it, and I've laid it out as a blogger as best I could these last days – these damaged and these improving days, 78 of 'em. All of it.

None of this was my idea. I imagine it fell out of me and fell through me and perhaps I 'spose as a result of me, but I did not and could not imagine it back there in the first place, some other Wednesday, when a life spirit with its own plans and schemes, jokes and dead seriousness's, said something like "Enough of this one" and said "How about this one?" and one's a statement and one's a question and in about 37 hours it'll be my car's tires doing the talking and I'll bring my best attention to the journey – a journey I'm pretty sure both of odometer and metaphor – and maybe 1000 miles away I will have some new ideas, they will be my ideas, I'll stand on a cliff above the Pacific and yell to it all — "This, this right here today, yeah, this is my idea.

But, like I told Noreen, it for sure wasn't my idea before.

July

Out loud

Lots of little things today. Dots at the ends of sentences – the sentences left, the ones I think of. The last hours.

Thursday, the first of July, covid apparently wanes, my marriage is over. I went out into Kate's back yard, under a spreading apple tree, and trimmed my beard and hair with the electric I'd bought and shared the cost of with Spenser back when the salon we went to off Powell in Portland closed with just about everything else. We used it a lot, and as his legally designated finance guy I bought him a brand new one to bring along to Aaron and Kalae's and I kept this one, and also I've carried the very early tomorrow-morning boxes of my most important things out to the car in dress rehearsal of the best possible packing and I'll bring them back in soon and put them here on the patio for easy grabbing. I've microwaved what could be my last cup of Oregon coffee, cooling as I type, no coffee in the morning, the bathroom calls more often in these eighth decade days and I'd like to get a couple hundred miles down the road before any stops. Ibuprofen will be handy for a likely looming headache.

I gassed the car after the early Encinitas zoom, and as it's not about me I said nothing about the next time I zoom them I'll be in their own backyard. Let's see how it goes. This pretty much presumes the creek don't rise and there ain't no meltdown and I make it safe down the 5 and 505 and 80 and 580 and the side streets of Oakland CA for a wicked fabulous reunion with Gavin, him who's held me up the most for 79 days, and his trusty sidekick Jen (quite affectionately called the Princess of Darkness, which will be a tale another day, from a more SoCal slant). And then on safely to just north of San Diego.

Since I do have a plan to come back to Portland in September and hang with Spenser a couple of days and have a U-Haul truck rented and waiting and strong young people to help me load my meager but sentimental collection of stuff out of Joyce's garage – no details presently reality-based – I won't say this is my last Blog post from Oregon or the last cup of coffee in Oregon or walking in circles and thinking about stuff in Oregon. But as an Oregon resident, which I've been the last 12 point something years, yes. I'm done.

Thanks for hanging in. I'm thinking no post tomorrow, the first Monday through a Friday I will have missed since I announced this plan back the third week in January. Some 700 miles between me and Gavin and the Princess and LaLa the pup will see to that. Who knows, I get the hang of Encinitas internet waves, maybe I'll sneak in a post over the weekend. Safe arrival thing. Crawling through a brand-new window once upon a time tale. Wide awake alert for the magic and wonder, and with possibly an owl flying along south with me, just off the freeway – spirit creature, friend of mine.

The morning program is get up with the crazy early alarm, pray on knees, meditate, and write my Morning Pages. Then boogie. The fact that there is an all-encompassing plan for me – a caring plan – and the Universe keeps smiling on me, these things are so clear now. Shiny edges to sad days, I'm hoping to rest in that wonder and joy, keep my eyes on the prize, mostly drive defensively, and rejoice getting to hang out in Oakland, and a day later, sit over the Pacific and says "Thanks."

Out loud.

So Much

I was explaining to someone from La Paz, Mexico this morning, a current housemate, that when I announced the third week in January of this year I was going to begin a daily Monday through Friday Blog post that what I would be reporting on any given of those days would be what I called "my daily weather". Here's todays:

I arrived safely and relatively psychotic in Encinitas late Saturday afternoon. Two days of insane driving – forest fires, endless stops and go's, tailgaters, brake-tappers, two lanes, five lanes, nice people and not-so-nice people, lots of truly bad scanning radio, and a final dead stop endless jam some 15 north of Encinitas driving me to flee the freeway to the coast highway and sit in red-light, tourists-are-us, when's-it-end last 40 minutes – two days of all that and noticing and rejoicing along the way with first palm trees and first eucalyptus trees and the entering "Irvine" sign and my favorite bougainvillea, and I was tired and 72-year old wrung out beyond imagination. I last did something this extreme 13 years before, geez, I was still in my 50's. I found the house where I'd rented a room – a room had been promised to me – and there was the owner, my new landlady you could say, and her friends from La Paz and they were on the way out to a party and I unloaded everything I'd scavenged from the divorce, not otherwise stored in Joyce's Portland garage, and got back in the car against all sanity instincts and drove to the ocean and took a couple of selfies to prove it to you and, yup, me too, then wandered what might be called Main Street on the lookout for a cheap Mexican place and a burrito, my third in four days and so much for no grain ever and the pledge of allegiance to Keto, and I accosted two young women who directed me to that joint and – no food all day – I wolfed down a veggie burrito and came back to my new "home" and got the laptop working and even the desktop working and took a Tylenol pm and crashed out.

It's a huge house with insanely beautiful tile work and my favorite-in-life succulent plants everywhere in a swirling never-ending yard and I've been filled with joy and out-loud counting my blessings and it hasn't been two days yet and this morning I vowed to myself to go to the ocean every day I'm here, and this morning the printer still wouldn't work (forever 'offline') and this morning I found I had 10 days to get a California license and 20 days to get Cali plates and I have no evidence of residence, no mail, no utility bills, and it's been a little funky between the landlady and myself and I keep reminding myself to be in the now and rejoice in waking up another day and me living a life-long dream – a life on the coast of California – and I thought I'd have the big exhale after finally arriving down this path which has been placed before me, knowing that's when the serious sadness of no longer having my wife, my soulmate, and having left my son (in angelic hands) would arrive to stay a while, but there is more to do and more to do with big deadlines looming and the landlady made a snarky crack which had me wondering how long I'll be here and, that's cool, because I'm here now and for sure through July 31 and then maybe a free place to stay for a couple of weeks if things don't work out here, though I may be so exhausted as to be clinically paranoid and me and the landlady may be toasting sparkling water as best buds four July 4ths from now. And this is my weather today. This is how I am today. Like I like to say to myself – right here, right now. Like Dick M was always telling me – right where I'm supposed to be.

I do not feel a need to be all warm and fuzzy this Monday

and I don't feel like I'm complaining either. Not really. I kind of thought there'd be something like the big exhale and a serious period of relaxing, but say la vie say the old folks, I guess you suit up and show up and do whats you gots to do, and with a heart filled with kindness and the ever-present gathering of grace, even with new and more stuff, here I am in Encinitas.

Living the dream.

And I Got

Today

I got interviewed. I got fingerprinted. I got stuck in traffic on the 5 (again). I got a sweet drive on the Ted Williams Freeway. I got to think about Ted.

I got ten thousand grand hummingbirds and butterflies and mourning doves. I got a cranky up-and-down morning walk (yuck) and a special, lovely beach-side one (yay).

I got my marching orders for a part-time Chance the Gardener house gig to help defray the real high cost of living – defraying just a smidge – and a job confirmation and a first assigned shift.

I got a ticking clock – license and reg, license and reg, license and reg – and perhaps a competent mechanic shop for every oil change the Camry wants. I got almost a full tank of gas, after $200 plus for gas the last four days.

I got a flock of Moonlight Beach pigeons, they swirl around and swing around and there's something Jurassic about it, and so cool when they pass inches above my barely-haired head. Oh, I got pelicans, a thrill for me. Bunches of gliding pelicans.

I got a sore back and a nearly-empty stomach and nowhere near enough Trader Joe's almond butter.

And like the 'Hair' song says – I got my ass. It's kind of funky. But I got it.

And I got something like six more hours – today – in which to count my blessings.

Oh – I got inspired to ask friends to write me letters too.

Fingers crossed.

Sweet

I had a phone call today. I made the call. It was a long call, and the person to whom I was speaking – no, make that begging for help – hung in the whole time. Second hand, minute hand spinning round and round. Doofus on this end of the line a technical no-nothing, and, yeah, that's probably a bit of stress in the voice of the usually no-stress kid. Blockages and defaults, following directions into a maze and – oh, yeah – there ain't none for back out. The woman on the other end, babysitting for sure, may have been the Buddha reincarnate, I honestly think so, sent back from the endless empty to remain anonymous amidst the depths of the "we-help-fools" section of Kaiser Permanente. Clocked in, different day, same old same old. And she remained patient beyond any expectation you'd ever have for a civil servant. For a human support worker. Pretty much for anybody – even your cousin, even your bestie. She apologized to me for my ineptness, I swear, saying "It's okay honey, we going to get you there. It'll be okay and even if we need to call in the big guns, the technology heavies who can peer with analyzing eyes into the very electrical innards of your desktop from a zillion miles away. I promise, darling, you gonna be alright."

Her name was Sweet.

"Thank you for calling Medicare enrollment at Kaiser Permanente today. My name's Sweet. How may I help you?"

Sign my sorry funky butt into Southern California health care coverage, mam. If you can.

And she could and she did, and it was righteous and it was sweet.

Catch the Wind

It's just beyond noon on this Thursday and I've done a few things for sure – early walk, all the morning routines, a zoom into Oakland, another shopping visit to Trader Joe's, a walk over to the Encinitas Senior Center where – here comes delusional me – everyone seemed older and with enough friends and acquaintances, and the program was about activities and not the kinds of supports I was hoping for, so a walk back to the new room (renting a room real weird in itself), and a long email to Maria in San Diego, she of the senior center who was so generous with her work days while I was doing time back in the basement in Portland, asking now for just a bit more help and direction.

There was a small breakfast in there too, and a bit more weeding and sweeping and watering the potted plants with a watering can, part of the deal here reducing my rent from horrifyingly high to my-hair's-on-fire high. Still. How lucky am I? I felt a presence encouraging me to make a move to San Diego, a week into losing my wife and my house and in a day-to-day way my son, and I turned all my attention to that encouragement and through the aid of forces beyond my tiny comprehension and the splurge of amazing generosity and kindness from so many good folks, I found a place – expensive but made available to me – just 25 miles short of downtown SD. Which, thinking about, feels remarkable and slightly mystical and without doubt amazing.

Yesterday and today, while still with long 'To Do' lists and pretty much continuing to be directly involved with life through all the moments of the day, it has been less of the frantic need to keep on keeping on and reply to post after post and sell myself as a cool dude in a loose mood every chance I got, and move and pack and lug, and not to forget the crazy 1000-mile drive. Most of all that is done. Here I am. Encinitas.

And what I knew was over there in the corner, waiting on the degree of nuttiness to subside, say okay this cat's ready to exhale and kick it some – what I always knew would come out from the shadows and sit directly beside me is, I miss my wife.

I've started having make-believe conversations with her. I've started reminding her that we came to Encinitas twice, and swam in that ocean right down there from where I sit on the overlook up here. I've thought about texting – How are you doing? About calling for just a quick hello. Wondering if she'd even answer. Just wanting to tell her stuff, all the stuff of the day, all the things I said so often and so matter-of-factly during all the days of all those years. I think it's just beginning, this empty space, and there's a part of me with the fear I'll never ever get a chance to talk with her again.

"To feel you all around me and to take your hand along the sand. Ah, but I may as well try and catch the wind."

It is gorgeous and magical and living a life-long dream being here. Right here. Here in Southern California. At the ocean. But, it's not all peaches and cream.

It Was Kind Of

interesting..

Mr. Baker's Parade

There was an old guy who used to walk by my growing-up house every day when I was a kid, when I was out in the yard. His name was Mr. Baker. He was wicked old. Seemed kind of ancient. If my flickering brain cells remember correctly, he was always wearing dressy clothes, I picture nice pants (old peoples' pants) and a sports jacket. He was, for sure, always wearing a hat, some kind of top hat, round with a brim. Mostly I remember his cigar. There was always a cigar. I couldn't tell you this morning if it was lit or not, I'm guessing it was, but ever-present was a cigar between his lips, making that daily journey with him.

I was thinking about Mr. Baker yesterday morning while out on a daily walk of my own – sans cigar – he showed up in my head along with my memory of what I experienced as his gentle uniqueness, and I had the thought, while walking, that now I'm a Mr. Baker. It's not the same small residential street like back there in Wareham, Massachusetts in the 50's and 60's. And his dressing up is my dressing down, me every morning with old shorts, a tank top of one color or another, NB running/walking shoes and white ankle socks. But I imagined that when I turned the corner off the busy Balour Drive with its fast-moving morning cars and trucks and made the left up the hill on Melba Road, that when I was passing house after house and possibly with Melba Road folks up and about at 6:25 and looking out the window, they saw this old guy walking up the road and a few minutes later back down it. And there he was again, yes, he passed last Thursday and last Friday and Saturday and Sunday too, "Right Honey?", and now again here Monday morning. While we get up and ready for work and our day, there's this old guy in a tank top passing up and back down. They just don't know my name is Mr. Cushman, how would they – I don't know anyone here. It's easier to say, "There he goes again."

I cannot imagine, back when I was nine or 11 or 13, thinking that'd be me some day, I'd be just like Mr. Baker, walking the same route pretty much the same time of the day, strolling along slowly and surely, and who knows what's on that cat's mind – anything at all? – the folks on Melba might wonder. But they'd only wonder for a moment. Life's lifey, and there's stuff to do.

I've been walking another everyday route here in Encinitas, California too, this one on the numbered streets – Second, Third, and Fourth – over next to the cliffs and up above the Pacific Ocean. It's my new favorite walk, those streets surprisingly not whizzing with cars, and, sure, they're just houses after houses and some apartment buildings and tourists condos and stuff side-by-side and mostly all the roads lead to the Moonlight Beach parking lot, just plain old streets, but there's something about being in the balmy sunny air and seeing big succulents and bougainvillea and flowers all over, already I feel amazingly blessed for having found it – having found my way all the way to here near San Diego. And showing up every day on the numbered streets, I guess if anyone's noticing, me being a Mr. Baker here and now. "Look, Sweetie, there's that older dude again."

My Mr. Baker may have traveled up one side of the country or across it to get there to my hometown of Wareham, or not, I'll never know. He was just the old guy walking by every day, looking real peaceable, like that same old same old walk was enough. Probably more than enough. He walked under Dutch Elms lining each side of High Street when I was young, though the Elms were gone by my high school days. Maybe Mr. Baker was by then too – I don't remember. Somewhere I stopped seeing and noticing him, and that could have been my new-found important growing-up busyness – versus him no longer there. Maybe not noticing enough of the real stuff anymore.

Anyway – it seems fun, to me, how things in this life sometimes go. Life's parade. Going around, coming around….

empty mind, filled mind

I come to the Blog today with empty mind. Swirls and whirlpools, gurgling noises from deep in the woods, the sound of a cloud passing overhead. I went out to the curving driveway here in the home in which I rent a room now – this is nine days – and with a push broom tired my arms out clearing endless pine needles, hoping that the focused effort might open a trap door in the old W.B. brain and let loose just a bit of daylight. I bet I couldn't tell you the difference either way.

Yesterday's Blog was a fun story about childhood days and getting older days and hats and cigars and homeowners glancing out their windows. Today it's different. Like a guy I know says – chop wood, carry water. It's kind of one of those days. Yesterday I arrived 15 minutes early in the parking lot of the young man I was being hired and trained to work with, and sitting in my car I texted my boss and told her not to bother showing with the high-tech iPad and iPod and double secret handshakes and all the documentary gadgetry, because on second thought – which was an extended long thought over the weekend – I'd had enough concerns about my abilities to perform – not that recording crap – but basic needs to help this young man remain safe and healthy, with his 24-hour seven-day nursing care and about 17 posted-on-the-walls schedules and formats and requirements of just what that day needed to look like for him. I'm sorry, like, lighten up, that's just not me and as I've been officially retired these last 10 years and will not make a decision to do something which brings me stress and discomfort and genuine concerns about me being the right guy, I told her (my boss) thanks for being one of the paths leading me to Encinitas, but this isn't me and why go in and hang with the guy another day – so he'd soak in my hipness – when I knew in my heart I wasn't going to come back.

So I called and asked her to read the text and she did and called back and said they didn't have anyone else who'd work better for me and thanked me for being straight with her early on (I may be an asshole in her young mind), and I drove back to the big house with my big, fairly empty room (my furniture stranded in a gracious garage in Portland) and I immediately began sending out resumes to some of the weirdest places for the weirdest work and went out with a legal pad and pen and sat in the balmy sun and wrote down everything I could think of to make money and to save money, and there were some very cool ideas and among them no guarantees, and I'm good down here for quite a while and a while can kind of be as long I vision it – when I live something like a Spartan and keep on keeping on reaching out to the Universe with that question of perpetual spirituality – "Now what?"

So, everything I did yesterday and everything I've done so far today, including re-juicing my Facebook Art Page and my Patreon Patron page and my Fine Art website page – it's all me chopping wood and carrying water. And – and I knew this back at the first sentence – empty mind is full mind. Plots, schemes, devotions, vast intentions, dreams and wishes, hopes and vows, always asking for help and always being kind enough to accept it, open arms and clear clarity about what feels right, going all-in and barely poking my toe into the ancient and rather chilly ocean. Empty – full.

My prayer is that I get a chance to do this all again tomorrow. Like they said back on WBCN back in Boston back in the day – If the creek don't rise and there ain't no meltdown.

The end of a scribble

…….and I did go outside earlier before brekkie and trim a lavender shrub which was clearly wild and out of maybe expected control – who wants to control nature, really, though nature is nebulous what with that being planted and water-drip maintained there, and anyway I hope the take is positive and will be bummed if it ain't, but here again I remind myself which I hope to every hour or two, the joy is in the journey, and it's all interesting, and I am amazed and pleased and thrilled just to have arrived here, and I live in Encinitas CA now and there are some people who seem to like me well enough already and I haven't even met anyone in person yet though that's coming, I feel it, and a coffee scheduled in a week or so with Peter R and I will hopefully be an exquisite listener and be there then – the "be here now" of the predicted event future – and see how it goes. And another thing is sending out resumes after punking (for good reasons) on the Downs job and the math of real numbers and chunks of existing savings diminishing and so I'm sending stuff out, resumes etc., and I'm putting myself out there all over the place with Craigslist posts and when I do that and like yesterday ask everyone already knowing me to consider my art as ongoing and future support, I likely too eagerly and pretty sure too often am back on the email hoping for newness and looking around, and checking the phone, and it would probably not be very human of me not to feel a smidge of disappointment when there's nothing there, no one home, but all I can do is all I can do and all I can do is keep working persistently and all-in, all the way with giddy joy and pleasure, to be there making shit happen on my side of the street. Only place for me, Brah!! And I dig it and almost always these days of sadness and longing and fabulous wonder and amazements, pretty much I'm doing the right thing most the time.

And here it is just after noon and I prayed and sat and drank coffee and wrote inspired notebook and steno pad notes and I walked up Melba and back and I zoomed myself into "no one kicked me out!!", and doing guerrilla laundry, and I trimmed the bush in the yard and I think it looks kind of cool – I'd defend the work as "different" – and suddenly all I'm smelling is lavender and maybe I'll have lavender dreams and maybe there's something there for me in the idea of lavender and I don't know, not much about nothing really, and there's the early boys and the very first group again and most of all I need to know, and Gavin dug my "Guru" post though apparently no one else has – yet…….

more local than before

I'm feeling like a local, here in Encinitas, CA, more with each day drifting by on the westerlies. Today I went and got my library card (I think there's a pic popping up here in a second). There's nothing like a library card, a free ticket to the fun house, to a world of visions and dreams and brain cell stimulation, and mostly for me it's just crazy good, a library, books for free and nowadays DVDs too, and a thrill for me this morning was walking into the low-slung building – all California-like – and straight across and through the wide expanse, out there through the glass – there's the endless blue of the Pacific Ocean. Like a hot dog with not only mustard and relish – but onions too. Jackpot.

Their computers were on the fritz but they managed me a card and I strolled around and walked out onto a balcony with fun chairs where you can sit and read and think about stuff – I bet – and there's the Pacific and it doesn't and didn't cost a thing other than five minutes to prove I'm me and I'm a resident (a local) here now and a woman named Honey hands me my plastic and I walk the aisles and land in fiction and head right to James Lee Burke and find a couple I don't remember reading yet, having read like 25 of his, and I take them out – via hand-written numbers with the computer glitch – and drive them home and I sat outside a while ago and read 29 pages of the first one.

Which, in addition to me being more of a local than ever, and now with my very own San Diego County library system card, is itself something because if you're a follower of Couch Surfing at 70 you may remember my chronic, devoted, daily immersion in books, one book after another, a couple started and finished each week – that aspect of my life coming to a crashing halt April 15, exactly three months ago, the day after I heard the word "divorce". I have been reading some Zen journaling since I got here, there's that, more healing maybe, but today was the first regular book.

I did some gardening out in the yard – part of the rental deal – and put my name into an agency looking for part-time work which generated a lot of clearly misplaced interest. So phone calls and good luck anyways. And all of it is happening here, 1000 miles south of that sadness and the divorce and the end to reading back there.

All of which makes me more of a local than, say last Friday. A surfer-dreaming boy in a SoCal beach town – with a library card of his own.

the good foot

This Friday was a slightly more "structured" day than I've had in a while. Like formal, distinct, specific things to do. Starting early was leading a Zoomy thing, kind of doing what I've done a few decades now, it falls nicely under the cute euphemism, "You've got to give it away to keep it."

Next up was a very formal, serious, matters-a-bunch, some-while-ago scheduled interview with a representative of the state of California regarding a couple of senior-and-broke-as-a-mongoose potential benefits I may be eligible for, which these days anything helps a lot and so fingers crossed electrically in hopes for the good word coming in another few weeks. Hoping to be hopeful is the interesting place of not wanting to set myself up, what (clearly) with no guarantees these days, and at the same time employing my powers of positive visualization to see the thing happening, to help make it real – not, I'll believe it when I see it, but, I'll see it when I believe it. Tightrope time, but the kid pretty much always leans into a keeping the faith, Baby, place. That government chat went on and on.

Lastly, among the "formal" obligations was a meeting with who would have been my ongoing boss had I not decided the gig begun/interviewed for back there in Portland turned out not to be right for me on all kinds of levels, and today (in front of Trader Joe's on the Boulevard – my choice) there was a matter of me signing something saying I'm outie and have no claims on nothing. I kind of like that.

Also, like always, there's a long collection of actions and needs and good ideas and inspirations and I gotta's and keep on keeping on's, Holmes, in today's "To Do" list, these three above being more formal and scheduled than most of what's been happening down here in SoCal since my arrival 13 days ago – amazing – other than an oil change and the interview for the job not to be. And so's you can continue believing in the kid, I'm planning to keep – as James Brown would say – on "the good foot" all day and later drive over near the ocean and do the walk on the numbered streets I have made my own and become one with and after sit on maybe the Virginia Krick bench high above Moonlight Beach and the Pacific and will myself onto the magical drifts and streams of pelicans and look out to the endless breaking waves and wonder if the state of California will see fit to lend an old guy a helping hand, and think about some of the stuff I said in the Zoom hours before, maybe me doing some helping there, also consider my age-72 job prospects, I'd like to do something which feels like helping the planet and – to be clear – best would be creating new art and publishing new books and sort of be my own boss and break even with money and even maybe take up surfing if I can find some free lessons and some shallow water.

That'd be me on just another good foot. Barefootin'.

Keep an eye on summer

Me being lazy, scoffing up one of my favorite Beach Boys songs for today's title. The Blog titles have seemed way less important lately, compared with the stuff.

Today, Monday, scooting past mid-July, I'm lazy and in fact have come here without my usual pizzazz to begin banging the keys with both index fingers and see what shows up. I'm kinda like the Blog readers – I wonder what this bozo's gonna lay on us today?

But this Monday I'm a little logy – I love that word, personally – logy – my wife used to laugh every time I used it but it was always flat-out electrically accurate as a describer to me. And I'm there today. Logy. (And wife-less)

However – I'm going to set the timer on my phone for five minutes in a sec and then just do the dodah and shine on like the crazy diamond I sometimes think/wish I am. Okay phone, five minutes. Go…….

My main man Keith, formerly of P'town, formerly of Malibu, currently brownstone-sitting in the West Village and selling his so unique and mystical art on a sidewalk table, he reached out via text way early this a.m. and asked would I like to help him get his first book of poetry published. I've been begging him to share one with the world for like forever, so it was a call-back and you damn skippy. He was selling at the time and we disconnected and a lady from San Diego County called with a follow-up call to one of the follow-up calls I've made regarding old-people benefits and can I receive any, please, as it is money out greater than money in, and remember a week back I rightly said adios to what would have been a pt-time job but coming back from the Keith and County lady talking walk, with beware rattlesnake signs – actually it said they have a right to be here too, they live here, and they'll leave you alone unless….ha, so I'm back and last night I sent this entirely goofy reply to a Craigslist post about a human service agency with positions, down in San Diego, and I've decided I'm going to copy and paste a post I currently have running on CL and you'll see what I sent which actually got me two replies today. All the more reason to know in my heart the Universe really and truly likes it when you stay active and alive and send all kinds of love and cool thoughts out into the nebula…

Five minutes.

Here's the copied and pasted –

Hello. I moved to Encinitas July 5 and would like to find a part-time position (10-12 hrs per week max) caring for an adolescent or young adult with a developmental disability, or a 'troubled' adolescent in a drop-in/outreach setting. I will be a welcome, positive, experienced contributor to/for any agency offering me an opportunity to serve. I am the father of a 28-year-old son with Down syndrome and the past two years have formally served in the capacity of personal support worker for him during and before the pandemic – employed through an Oregon state Brokerage within the developmental disability system (United Cerebral Palsy). Also trained by the SEIU union. Additionally, I have a 30+ year career in human services, serving in a variety of positions, both administrative and direct service, for a number of non-profit agencies, including residential treatment and housing programs for both adolescents and adults. A real strength is my ability to develop quality, genuine relationships with the people I serve. I believe strongly human services need to emphasize the human. Helping to provide – through a caring and respectful relationship – a space for individual growth and increased self-esteem. For a bigger, more joyful life.
I have excellent references, resume upon request, and a Bachelor's Degree in Social Welfare.

Still – pretty logy.

Being here now

Let me speak quickly to you today, internet chicanery is afoot, you'll find me now out on the patio, in search of the at times diminished at times entirely gone signal from whatever service the homeowner/landlady buys, I'm in the sun and it's quite lovely, the ambiance of this Southern California late afternoon, me with a still damp bathing suit, up from the wavy shallows of the Pacific where I instilled myself a while ago…….

after the Camry passed the required California Smog test, making tomorrow's trip to the DMV that more optimistic. After two telephone job interviews, in back-to-back succession, first with a supervisor, next with the CEO, some self-help outfit down in San Diego I mentioned yesterday, me with the goofy and lazy reply to their post seeking help and here comes three emails last night and two phone discussions, kind of interviews today and it may look good for the kid, maybe the chance to serve somebody with kind-hearted deeds remains, maybe the money in cozies back toward the money out. After an early Oakland zoom out here cause there was no electrics working in there, yup, after the internet stopped entirely on my desktop, a flat-out deal-breaker and I was once again in the got to move mode and then I was involved in two cool interviews and then the Camry passed with flying colors and then I was bobbing in the Pacific – like Brian Wilson wrote, like a cork on the ocean.

And I'm back here and there ain't no internet in my most expensive room, where I figured I ought to be given a free computer, what with that cost, and it's okay sitting out here even if my old back is bended unfortunately funny, and in a sec I'll hit "Publish" and see if it does, after typos are repaired, and the attitude toward my logging-in problem from housemates is blazay (cool spelling) at best and I honestly don't know what I'm gonna do, but it's so interesting I'm way down here – under the sun, cool in the ocean – trying to understand what's the next right thing.

trades we get

The brief post in my mind the last hour or so was this – "I ain't got the internet, kids, but I've got the California tags." I even took a picture, sitting on the driveway, when I arrived 'home' from the DMV, about 18 miles and 43 traffic jams up and down the road from Oceanside.

Then I went to speak to the landlady about the no internet and what can we do, and at that very moment she was on the phone with T-Mobile, her provider, 'cause the whole house, it turns out, was internet funky, not just the hip new kid way back there in the far room behind thick walls which – now they tell me – is historically a wide-web black hole. Anyway, the landlady was given the cosmic remedy – turn the router off and on – and the internet floated back on electron music into the house, even back there with the new kid, though buffering remained (and remains) a way of life. Why I'm out here on the patio again, struggling with the daylight and grateful the ability exists to make another weekday post.

Actually hanging in the DMV a couple of hours may have been a smidge better than my angst of the trouble with what seems so natural nowadays, pretty much zooming anywhere in the world. And it cost a lot less to register the Camry in California than it did in Oregon. Life's funny sometimes.

Anyway, not much in the couch surfer's mind today. In need of a chill pill, pretty clear on that, and again it's lovely in the external weather'd Encinitas milieu and humming-birds tick and chatter in the glorious yellow flowers directly behind me. And I have it as a goal to become more comfortable with the laptop in general, and using it out here more specifically. Maybe that's a be careful what you wish for, maybe old man river just keeps rolling along, oh, here's a flash, I have an interview for potential employment next Monday late afternoon, someplace called San Marcos. Hope I get to look up how to get there.

Thanks for hanging in, Blog devotees. Cosmic stimulation lately, via moi, on the down low.

times here now

(The following lifted from a today practice writing 25:25 session.)

"I wish I had it in me to write the Blog right now and maybe I do, maybe the sitting here and tap tap tapping the keys with an index-ian dexterity will wake something up in the ole brain cells, could happen, and it'll be copy and paste time kids and the deed complete yet one more weekday and I will (ceremoniously, in my mind) fall on my knees with big thanks and gratitude, a behavior becoming more familiar and part of the daily milieu, sort of like ritual, with each passing day. That, clearly, a good thing, the act of saying thank you, and I suppose there are antecedents to little kid prayers like lots of us were taught – Protestants anyway, can't speak for the Catholics – and being grateful and politely asking for more blessings, which gets to be a lot of blessings doing it every night, and anyway, I am a grateful guy and on less often occasions these days I can stray off the gratitude beam, and sometimes I do, and it makes me sad and no doubt it makes me unnecessarily suffer – and here I recall my first call-him mentor Dick M. always saying to me 'Your Higher Power didn't bring you this far to suffer', and say that's true, then it stands that any suffering I'm doing is by invitation only, my invite, and there is good news and that's the rare strays away from consistent awareness of my blessings, those straying times are fewer and farther between – why they stand out so dramatically – and are noticed by me much quicker, and quicker with every – say – month I'm allowed to keep waking up and showing up on the planet."

And then…..

"…and anyway I haven't found the spark to get me back in the chair before the keyboard making cool stuff up and I sure hope I do soon, there's no wife to devote my time to, no son to chase around the house and watch a zillion movies with, and yes it's possible I may find myself with a two-day-a-week job in the next few weeks, more to be revealed following Monday's interview, the point is this is the absolutely right time and place to return to my writer's ways and in fact go beyond where this Buddy has gone before and be one of those all-in, true writers and wake up ready to go and put in three or four or five hours ever day, maybe skip Saturdays, and just pour myself out onto the keyboard and the electric screen, oh, there's so much waiting on me.

"So this is a big wish of mine now, learning to surf a smaller wish and having enough money coming in to get close to the money going out and keep on being a big walker and keep on being braver than before and be kind and treat animals and insects kindly and if I get to work with humans again, always – always – keep my eyes on the prize which is how do I help someone (s) have a bigger, better, more full and joyous life? What else is human services for? So, ramble on space cadet and there's a ton of stuff on my four or five various-size try-for-these-things-pads of paper and one today says swimming and it was cloudy and now it's brightened up and it's 1.9 miles to the beach and ocean, though maybe another mile away catching a legit parking place, of course me with Cali plates now looking like a local for sures – I can see myself chatting up some surfer dudes, like, 'My homies, back at Venice Beach in the 60's you couldn't imagine the times, kooks and locals and the beginning of things, so always exciting', and think of it I'm right in the beginning of things again, 1000 miles from the life I was living and knowing and the girl I was so crazy in love with, and now look at me, Cali plates and a room I can afford awhile and every single day/night since I got here July 3 over at the beach as a sun and surf worshiper, up on the cliffy, benched overlook in honor of the Universe giggling in my direction, and maybe others are better at telling when there are gifts all wrapped up in what appear to be sorrows and shitstorms, I'm better than before I guess (though the divorce word fooled me a whole bunch), yes, I'm way more at one with the Vonnegut line that 'Strange travel suggestions may be dancing lessons from God', so I guess I'm dancing my older days away now, and I wouldn't mind trying the stroll as the dance of choice the next few days."

Can you dig the stroll?

when I was a king

When we were kids, us from one, maybe two streets, we'd play in our yards, backyards, front yards, sometimes we'd ride three-speed bikes on tar sidewalks, maybe down the middle of the street, daringly, possibly all around the big block of High Street and Main Street. Adults would see us, looking out from behind windows, maybe in lawn chairs, and they would say, "Look at those kings."

Often our dogs would play with us too. As our friends. As our companions. As our equals. Smarter than us. You'd look at them and say thanks for being friends and they'd stare that unwavering stare of devotion, and they were royals as well.

Sometimes, when I've been being all kingly and such, people have sought me out, they've come to where they knew I was – an apartment, a coffee shop, a guidance office. Or they'd call – knowing my number; knowing my area code. They came to me because they wanted me to tell them they were better than they felt they were. They knew I 'd tell them they were because I had before. I always had. And they knew I always would. I'd say, "You're a blessing." I'd say, "You're a gift." I'd say, "Ain't no one like you but you." I would hold up my kingly mirror, it affirmed their special, and I'd scrunch around and get a sideways glance at their direct-ahead stare, and I'd say, "See, I told you. So much to give, everything to share, to let the world in on." And they would say "Thank you king" and head home, or back to work, or back to second period.

Kings know accepting is more kingly than giving – I know that, being a king again – and I say yes and thank you and you go, girl and right on, bro, and I sit in the backyard with butterflies, I sit on the bench high above the ocean, I sit with a coffee in a straight chair and I see the wonder of it all. And I think, how royal of me.

Kings are always counting their blessings.

Encinitas is on the west side

I'm about to leave on a job interview. This interview was set up by the CEO of a non-profit agency down near the San Diego airport. The interview will be in a town called San Marcos, exactly 10 miles inland north and east of Encinitas. I'm to be interviewed by a young married couple – it's pretty much about them – and both sets of their parents. Six people, in someone's living room. People I've never met, in a living room in which I've never been, in a town I don't know.

I confess to being a little scared. Better pronounced skay-erd. Just a little. I'm also reminded of multiple conversations I've had with my best pal and long-time wicked smart mentor Gavin in Oakland, it's always me saying to him how life provides us over and over with opportunities for guerrilla theater. Colorful, in-your-face guerrilla theater opportunities. Like this one. See, the goal of guerrilla theater is to go way out of your way making a point, you give exaggeration a big new name, and if you do it right it's cool and hip and maybe causes a chuckle or two and generally lightens things up. Even with serious things.

In this case, my goal as a life-long member of the guerrilla theater troupe of national bozos will be to demonstrate flamboyantly and with wicked pizzazz that hiring me is the exact right move – none finer. During the interview I promise to be courteous and pleasant, polite and humble, a darling of the "Isn't he sweet" society. Just do it kind of loudly. Honestly, faithful readers of this Blog, I don't have anything else left. I don't. And it will go how it goes. Perhaps one parent doesn't like me and the other five do and I get the job. Or three parents don't and the kids and one of the moms do and I don't get the job. (You know how that goes.) Or maybe nobody likes me and I do not get the job.

Either way, the next day, tomorrow, Tuesday, it's likely I'm going to get a call from the CEO – her name's Beth – and she's going to say you're in like Flynn, when can you begin? Or she's going to say hit the road Jack and don't you come back no moe no moe…Or something in between. And I'll have I job, and I don't when I'm typing this. Or I won't and things will have remained the same, other than a few members of the planet being entertained with another episode of "Guerrillas in our Midst".

But, wait, think about this. In a few hours I will have had my second job interview here in greater San Diego in just over three weeks. Freakin' amazing. I can already hear Guinness calling – "Most failed job interviews by a 72-year-old gypsy having recently moved 1000 miles with a broken heart."

So. No matter what. It's like the song goes – "Something's coming, something good."

dignity of risk

I don't believe I've ever heard those three words put together, in that particular order. But I did this morning.

Oh, regarding Monday's post, I guess I passed the

collective eyes and ears of yesterday's interviewees because the CEO lady called me late last night and said words to the effect of "Welcome aboard, Kid." (I like it when people call me kid, there's a youthful, invigorated fragrance to it, so I made that part up.) But the word "welcome" was real.

Which had me this morning immediately bounced into a just-happened-to-be-scheduled-today quarterly agency orientation for new employees (part two this Friday), and it was a trip to be back in a human service orientation, and I swear I could not have sat here and index-finger tapped out words on the keyboard which would have made my heart smile more than the ones I heard today. No finer dialogue. Just wonderful and kind, and shining the light of possibility and joy on the word "human." And within the presentation were those three words – Dignity of Risk – on a slide in the Zoom and spoken by, call him, the Director man. And explained that there is great dignity in allowing folks, any someone, to try and reach for their stars, just theirs, the ones they cherish and some nights fall asleep to. The biggest ones. The going for it.

And I have to tell you – and regular readers of Couch Surfing at 70 already know – that doing things which feel right – honest to God, deep down, soul right – is the avenue I tend to walk more than not. Not worried about who's gonna say what, who's gonna try to pull me back, get all logical and with the "You can't do that's and the "Are you nuts?" and "Are you ever going to grow up?" Like they might have asked Peter Pan that.

Because a few hours ago I was in a room I somehow rented from 1000 miles away, here in the beach town of Encinitas, California, with an agency out of my right-now blue, them seemingly not giving a rat's ass about my birth certificate, and saying welcome aboard (Kid), come along with us, we're all about helping people to have bigger, more joyous, anything's possible lives. And now you – however it is you got here – well, you got here. Why don't you come along with us. There's a bunch of cool cats and kitties waiting for us to see what they need, and can we maybe help some.

My wife divorced me back in April and one morning amidst the clatter and distress of my broken heart risk poked its head through a newly-opened window in the me-of-me and asked if maybe I felt like taking another ride. Like getting in the car again. And, with circumstance playing a leading role, I said okay and then so many of you reading this came running down the streets of my past and my career and my circles of similar souls and offered your help. So much help.

Dignifying my risk one more time. Which, it seems now, I'll get to do some more of.

Paumalu

I put a $15 check in an entirely funky mailbox this morning, there on US coastal Highway 101 in Encinitas. The check was made out to Paumalu Press and snugged in an envelope addressed to a PO Box in Haleiwa, Hawaii.

Back in 2015 when I was married and my wife and I had enough accumulated Alaska Air miles to travel for twenty-six bucks each, round trip Portland to Honolulu and back, we did that and rented a small suv and drove from the airport up to Oahu's North Shore to a small apartment/cottage we'd rented through one of the on-line "rent me" sites. For eight days. It was a swell time, special, and we swam almost every day in Waimea Bay and drove back and forth on the Kamehameha Highway and sat on the lanai and drank morning and sometimes afternoon coffee and the sunsets were sweet and rainbows appeared often and it was a vacation – my only time there – and maybe you winced at the cost of food and gas and most everything and then paid it gratefully. It was Hawaii.

On the sixth day, I'm pretty sure, I did something – with big encouragement from the wife – I'd wanted to do my entire life, beginning way back there in the front yard in Wareham, Massachusetts, age 14 and crooning my best Beach Boys' imitations to getting around and driving my woodie and, most of all, being one of the everybody going surfing. I paid ninety dollars for a surf lesson at a local surf shop, there on Kamehameha in Haleiwa, and got there early, and after a while this woman showed up looking all laid back and surfy and she was my instructor and her name was Karen and we put a couple of boards from the shop in the back of her really beat pick-up truck and got me some kind of swim shirt to hopefully prevent skin from peeling off and the three of us crowded in the cab and traveled to a local spot and after a while of on-land instruction and advice and warning Karen and I paddled out. She'd said the hardest part would be the paddling and she was right, I only lasted about 20 minutes before heading back in, Brian Wilson no doubt somewhere in the background shaking his head. Remember. "It's a genuine fact that surfers rule."

I got up on the board just once, on a very small wave and only for a few seconds. But there and then I was a real gone daddy, living the life, blessed beyond all get out, and still with all my skin.

On the way back to the shop Karen said she had to make

a quick stop and we swung by the house where she lived with I'm pretty sure a bunch of other people and she ran in a minute and when she came out she said she'd had to do something for the magazine. And I asked what magazine – me being the writer I am, us writers all in it together and everything – and she said it was a magazine she published herself and pretty much thought up herself and directed herself and got some help with articles and photos, her gist being the north shore of Hawaii is a sacred place and I'm going to do everything I can to keep it that way. Spotlight on developers and encroachers, polluters and – well, it's an old story. This was her version.

It turns out the magazine was the Paumalu Press, just $15 for a year's subscription or some amount of every three-or-four-month editions, and I gladly, and gratefully, handed over the money. Then I said thanks for the thrill – thanks for dignifying my dream – and she left to do her Karen Hawaii thing and Susan and I left to finish out vacation and fly home, and back in Portland a few months later there came into the mailbox a fresh, gorgeous copy of the Paumalu Press. And they've been coming once in a while ever since, and this morning I found a hopefully still working mailbox on 101 and dropped a check in to Karen, with a note that future editions need to come here now, to Encinitas. Things stay the same, like the surf, and things change too.

It's okay today. Life seems rich when I go all in.

Too Busy to Weep

Last Sunday night, in a 1000-mile phone call, I told my friend Kate I'd been too busy to weep. In the three months since my wife had told me she wanted a divorce I'd wept twice – once after sitting behind my son Spenser, watching him take his t-shirts, one by one, and hand them to me for storage. There must have been more than 200, we only got to a few that day before he said enough, and it broke my heart and I went down to the basement and wept. The other time was when my wife came down to the basement to have a discussion about the business of saying goodbye and it ended with her saying something about our situation. She went upstairs and I thought about our situation and I wept.

Otherwise, like I said to Kate, I was too busy to weep. Finding a safe, loving space for Spenser. Finding a place for me to live, staying in Portland no option. Lugging books and furniture and bags up and down and out and into a friend's garage, trip after trip across town. Answering what felt like 10,000 Craigslist posts about rooms for rent, posting my own, changing this word and that so hopefully to better engage. Asking for help over and over, having to be okay accepting the help. Transitioning Spenser to his new home, trip after trip up there and back. Crashing with a friend a month. Connecting up with people I didn't know over and over in hopes one or more would be able to help. Applying for jobs 10 years after retirement, zoom interview, paperwork and CPR certification. Busy, busy, busy.

I was too busy to weep. Then I got to Encinitas and the job fell through and there was way more money going out than coming in and I'm trying to arrange health care and automotive care and California citizenship and plates and a license. But mostly settled and the kid safe and sound back in Oregon. And Sunday I had a long talk with an old-time friend who'd sent me a lot of money to help, being my friend, and we talked about a big sense of loneliness I'd felt the day before – knowing no one here. And we talked about my wife, and this huge hole in my life, my best friend gone, my soulmate, and loneliness being lonelier than ever before – ever in my life. And he said get ready, it's coming, and the only way through is time.

And Sunday afternoon I wept, and then again Monday and then again Tuesday. Not so busy. More room, and time, for grief.

Now my computer has crashed three times today – fatal error messages. I don't know if this will make it to post. I've been trying to catch up to all kinds of little things today, paperwork and internet work and stuff and life changes. I think I'll leave it here, still busy with life, differently, no choice but to give time time.

Walk, walk, walking

I've been thinking about something these last few days and it's been reinforced (or maybe ignited) by the two orientation trainings I've now sat through with the new agency. I thought I'd write about it today, last day of the week, and I went on an extended beyond the usual walk in hopes the post would fall out verbatim into my head – the way it often does when I walk – and I'd come back to my room and transcribe each word and possibly even include visuals. It was a good plan.

Then I went on the walk and what fell out is I'm not ready to write about this particular thing. I haven't given it enough thought, I have not paid enough attention. Not enough dues. Not yet. I'll get to it when I'm supposed to and that will be, I think, when I get 'it' more. Do you get that? In fact, right after I hit the publish button up there on the top right I'm going to do what I love doing and take my yellow legal pad and a blue medium pen and find someplace comfortable to sit, turn the timer on my phone for, um, 13, and write down every single thought which comes into my head about what it is I do not get enough just yet. And spend a lot of this weekend, I have a feeling, keeping on keeping on thinking about it.

So – here's to you for taking a couple of minutes to check in – a true thrill for me when I know someone's reading here – and I hope it is a great remaining Friday and gentle and hopeful and energizing weekend. For me, I'll try my best to be at one with this Ojibwa notion:

"Sometimes I go about in pity for myself, and all the while a great wind is bearing me across the sky."

Peace out.

the grade

I like the movie "School of Rock". I like it a lot. It's been a joy for me many years sitting with my son Spenser and watching "School of Rock". He likes it even more than me. We've had a lot of fun together – knowing the next line, singing the next song. One-upping each other's "School of Rock" knowledge. Cool father and son time.

I have a favorite line in the movie, in which there are many really good ones. But this one is my favorite. It's spoken by the character named Summer, she of the 'Class Factotum' pedigree, if you've seen the movie, you know who I mean. Kind of uppity and slightly holier than thou, a tinge of arrogance. What about our marks, what about our futures? That's when we meet her. Now, everyone goes through changes in the movie, surely Jack Black who goes from scamming for rent money to genuinely falling for the kids. But it's the change Summer goes through which I dig the most. Why she has my favorite line, Led Zeppelin's "Immigrant Song" yowling in the background, Jack letting her know he's going to fulfill her wildest dreams and give her "an A plus and 50 gold stars" for engineering the trickery the rocksters have just pulled off to be offered entry into the battle of the bands. But surprise, and finally – here's the line: "I didn't do it for the grade."

I didn't do it for the grade. I didn't do it to get something out of it for me. I had no personal agenda. It's not about me. It was just the right thing to do. That's why I did it.

Summer didn't say all those things, just the "not for the grade" part, but the message is implicit. I did the right thing, and because it was right that's why I did it.

Today is my (ex) wife's birthday. I sent her a text early this morning, saying I hoped it was going to be a wonderful day for her. That's all. As badly as I have missed her, that emptiness growing over time, especially powerful and painful last week, I wanted to tell her happy birthday. I got to spend the last 11 with her. And now not this one.

For a lot of the years of my life, and most often unbeknownst to me, my behaviors were directed by what I could or would get out of something. When I began getting a clue about how I was built, how I worked, I got to start owning my own and making changes toward a healthier me. It's been a lot of work, and worth it all. To go from self-centered-ness to, most of the time, other-centered-ness. The last couple of months I have ached, literally ached, to hear my (ex) wife's voice. Just to have her talk to me. But it hasn't happened even once, and it dawned on me on an early walk today, right after sending the text, the old me would have sent it in the hopes it would be enough to jiggle some compassion and for old-times-sake out of her and get a phone call. Like, surely this reaching out deserves a reply. On today's walk I thought about it and I was clear I'd sent the text because I just wanted to say happy birthday. To the closest person in my life for a lot of the years of it. Just say I hope it's a wonderful day.

Today, I'm like Summer. I didn't do it for the grade.

Tuesday afternoon

I was sitting in the Camry in the Moonlight Beach parking lot high above the Pacific Ocean last night, around 7:30, in conversation with my main man and ongoing mentor Gavin in Oakland. We were in agreement, the both of us, that I was doing a better job of living my life more fully these days – as in, way closer to the goal of "all-in" I'd been pleading with myself for years and years to get to. Yes, I'd go all-in here and there, this writing project, channeling that abstract painting, surely listening fully when the wife needed to talk. Only fragments of time. But there would be so many days – even with my life filled with blessings and me aware of them – when I let my head fall down to the pillow I'd think there was a lot more I could have got done that day. And would have if only – my ageless lament – I could find the way to suit up and show up entirely 100 percent, giving everything.

Last night, contrarily, Gavin and I were of the conclusion that I'm way more all-in these days, living each hour of each day with more devotion. More commitment. Way more observation that my life seems interesting, and, yeah, some of the time with more abandon. Kind of a dream come true.

Bursting into tears right there on a stone bench in public on a Sunday afternoon – now, that's living life more fully. More completely. Not just talking about sadness, not even just writing about it – living it right out loud, feeling it all the way, internal mercury bubbling up into the red. And ditto for walking down the middle of the road because tar's better than concrete and there's less of a lip in the muddle and a stoned surfer dude passing on his bike yelling "you're down the middle man" and me giving up the peace sign and knowing that there's a freedom I'm feeling which is different. Man, I'm in a road 1000 miles away from where I had the most wonderful life, and I'm under royal palms versus Douglas firs, and I'm all alone – entirely alone – and not with the love of my life. And I see older couples walking and laughing and being so happy and I start to cry and I listen to sad songs and I weep on a new cue. And I stand in front of my favorite bench high up there above the Pacific and bow to the ocean and bow to that one palm in the middle of the beach, I bow to that huge succulent garden just over there near Fourth and to that crazy grove of palms and that team of pelicans passing, just passing. I don't give a thought to if anyone's looking and I don't care, and I've been to an insanely fabulous job orientation to a job I'm about to begin at age 72 because I cannot afford to sustain this beach- town life very long with the rent and the social security and that goofy math and I ain't afraid – I am not afraid – people have held me up, people have urged me on, people have rushed to my side, they've formed a human safety net, and I know I'm taken care of and the Universe, it looks down on me with a silly old grin…

And what I wanted to say is I gave nearly every bit of my art supplies away in the move from my marriage and Portland and now am buying small bits back and this morning I set up the acrylic paint keep-it-fresh palette and pulled out the best of the old brushes I tucked in a bag deep in my trunk 1000 miles ago, and the few acrylic tubes, and I have no studio and I have no table even on which to put my stuff, I do have the $29 folding easel I first bought back when someone I knew suggested trying painting for fun and I couldn't tell you at all how it's going to work, how I become an active artist again – but I'm gonna – and the fact is I'll really be hoping to sell some of my new creations to help out with all the math of my Encinitas, Pacific-Ocean beach-side didn't ask for it life, and I go to bed early every night and get up way earlier than most everyone and these days I'm writing my Morning Pages and a timed writing and a weekday Blog post, I'm back to writing three times a day and I do have two of my dust-covered stories up to re-read and maybe edit a little and hopefully get charged to get all-in with my story-telling again – it's who I am – and lots of time the computer's buffering and I've been told it keeps crashing cause it's freakin' old – like you Pops – and I'll probably need to find money for a new cheap computer and maybe even a modem and router right here in the big and lonely and still magical and pretty mystical room I was lucky to rent, where the internet sucks,

And all of it means it's Tuesday afternoon and I'm kind of buzzing with possibilities and with brightly burning emotions and I'm planning on jumping in the Pacific in an hour or so and out loud giggle and thank my lucky stars and turn around and look at that palm up there on the beach and say something like, "Holy shit. Look at me now."

Maybe this makes no sense, except it does to me, which is

a place I find myself in all the time these days, and it has to be okay, and it mostly is. The feeling all-in part – that's really cool.

Ain't no use

This is one of those few days – both the computer and the beams of internet clinging to life – when I come to the Blog at Couch Surfing with nothing to say. Not one thing. Nothing serious, nothing heavy, nothing remorseful, witty, far out, earth-shaking, resentful, fabulously grateful, amazingly stupid, charming, bashful, low-self-esteemed, cool, remarkable, even run-of-the-mill.

Nada.

In "Don't Think Twice" Dylan sings "You just kind of wasted my precious time." And I know your time is indeed precious and I for sure don't want to go wasting any of it – today at least – so,

I'm about to head out on a walk I've discovered and taken as my own, it's already feeling a smidge sacred – where I have to climb up three truly wicked uphills to get to the relatively flat top-of-the-cliff-side dirt/Torrey pine needle path which rambles on and from which you can see five different southern California mountain ranges on a clear day, to which today is more like a second cousin. Maybe the walk will provide me with blogging material wildly exciting and incredibly useful for your consideration, but, alas, this will already be here. And if I am truly lucky enough to wake up again tomorrow, just waking up such a blessing, then I'll start all over again paying my best attention to check on what's what on a Thursday.

The end.

Lines

There's a line from a Mose Alison song – "My mind is on vacation, but my mouth is working overtime." It might be relevant, in shape-shifting evidence – to this post. It reminds me, a little, of another line which was once upon a time heard here and there amidst gatherings of the don't-drink-one-day-at-a-time folks – "The monkey may be off my back, but the circus is still in town."

I have no theory for you, or evidence, that either of these fun statements are entirely relevant to my internal weather here in Encinitas, California this late Thursday morning. My mind does not feel on vacation, it's quite busy at work considering and planning, day-dreaming and scheming, wishing and hoping, I think mostly wondering. Now what? Now what happens? How long do I feel like this? When can I feel like that? How badly do I feel like I need something to spend the money it takes to get it? And why do I forget the astounding generosity of friends and acquaintances and that I'm flush, sort of, and have enough today? Never mind, in fact, I'm still here, the fact I was capable of opening my eyes and sliding out of my bed this morning – one more time – not only the biggest blessing going. It's mind-blowing. It's remarkable, a mystical gift I continue to get to chase the joy in the journey. However it looks.

I began taking bids again today for moving my stuff from Joyce's garage in Portland to my room down here – talk about the circus in town – and I also actually received a text from my ex-wife a while ago, that fact making me so happy in the ongoing silence of not knowing how she is, the content of which making me sad because I get reminded how it is. There's just so much – like they say in Al-Anon – the bitter with the better. And what my main man from way back when – Frenchy the longshoreman from Charlestown – was always saying – "I don't know nothing about nothing."

Lots of quotes, lots of swirling thoughts, I had the chance to meet in person earlier two people I have come to like a lot through the electric magic of Zoom, and in 15 minutes I'm heading out into the hinterlands where I've never been to have a coffee at the home of another. None of whom live in Encinitas, so none to hang out with here, where I live now, me contributing to the circus in this town. At 7 tonight I'm signed up for a Meet Up "writer's workshop" – a different attempt to meet people – which is yet another Zoom thing and there's only two people going beside me and I did write a cool story with the prompt which was sent out, and, yeah, I have pretty much decided to spend some of the money people gifted to me on things I do need.

"Sunday night arrives without a suitcase." Isn't that a line from a Beatles song? It's another line and feels as relevant as any of the others.

salt mines part 2

I met for a couple of hours this morning with my new boss at the Pannikan coffee shop, rapidly becoming a favored space for me – here in Encinitas. This was a get-the-paperwork-done get together, along with some final pieces of orientation – how to's for record-keeping and record-sharing, apps to be downloaded on the phone, time sheets, and where to park. Oh – be a very patient listener.

I was given my initial schedule. Shadow shifts Sunday and Monday, two and three hours respectively. Then my soon-to-be regular Tuesday 11a to 6p shift. Alone. With the kids. Expecting (the kids), no doubt, some level of knowledge from me about how best to provide support, like, hope he's not a dumbass. The kids being a young married couple, both with Down syndrome, been together now longer than my wife and I were. So, hearing they wanted me, they the agency, they the team of parents and workers and, mostly, they the kids, and hearing it becomes really real next Tuesday – um, four days from now – I experienced a slightly electric mix of thrill and fear. A wow and a yikes intertwined. It didn't have anything to do with the coffee.

I'm 72, I retired almost the day I could 10 years ago, and I'm going back to work because the money going out here on this brand new, crazy and unexpected path is way more than the money coming in. Being a paid employee obviously addresses that. But it's not the only reason. The chance to help someone – in this fortunate case, someones – live their most wanted and hoped-for life, the one they dream about like I dream about mine and I bet you dream about yours, man, I feel lucky. Maybe after a couple of consecutive seven-hour shifts (Mondays and Tuesdays) and I fall into an 18-hour coma of exhaustion, well, come see me then. But even that, becoming all used up for all kinds of right reasons, like I said, it's a really good deal.

If you are a regular here you know my youngest son has Down syndrome and that he made the decision to remain up in the Portland area with cool, hip, young people he loves – and who could blame him – and now here I find myself 1001 miles away and my path brings me to these kids. Something slightly amazing about it all.

Some early-morning presence announced itself to me about a week after my wife said she wanted a divorce, and there was clarity in my mind – right then and there – I should go to San Diego. I think you know that story. I turned my full older-guy energies and intentions and even cosmic spells on making it happen and I landed, with unending gracious help, 25 miles up the coast. I believed then and kept believing after I got here this was some planet equilibrium for indescribable sadness. A taking care of me. The last week or so, however, I've started having the funny feeling that maybe there's more to it than that. Maybe I was led all the way down here for a purpose which had and has less to do with my comfort. My joy. More making use of me as a channel. The me of me.

We'll see. I'll head back to the salt mines in a couple of days and I reckon I'll begin to find out. No doubt, it's gonna be a trip.

giving time

There's a saying – give time time. I know it and I do remember it. Then I forget it. Then – oh yeah – I remember it again. And then I forget it. Again.

Maybe that makes me an outlier. Maybe that makes me normal. Falling out of consciousness that things take time. Changes take time. Grief takes time, and even a fountain of joy and hope. That takes time to gather, time to acknowledge. Time to hang onto.

On a walk this morning it dawned on me that it took me four months to find a job when I moved to Portland, back there in '08. It's taken me five weeks here. It no doubt took me a long time to come upon people – or they come upon me – who became friends or confidants or reflections of just enough. It hasn't happened here yet, but I imagine it will. If I only remember to give time time. I've been desperately lonely and it really hasn't been that much time. Grief has come running to me, maybe it sauntered up, all of a sudden it was very large and powerful, and friends on the phone let me know you ain't seen nothing yet. Just give it time. And the healing part too, which for me right now feels a million miles away. I don't know. Possibly there will be healing, in time.

Three months ago I had no place to live. And no job to pay for one if I found it. Now I do (a room) and I have very mixed feelings about it, and a couple of days ago – when I was flying from one mood to another – I said to myself, "Let's see how it goes." It feels like some of the best advice I've heard from anyone – especially me – in a while. And it's got some of that time time quality to it.

There's so much evidence in my life lately that amazing things can happen, they do happen, and reminders no one's getting excused from the other stuff. Time tells.

If you come across me, and that happens primarily here and through my writing, and you find me whining, frustrated, frightened, angry, dumbfounded, ever, even for just a split-second, looking upon "Now what?" as a bad thing, please do me a favor. Tap my on the shoulder and say something like, "Yo, couch surfer, gtt." It will be appreciated.

today

My life, today, is filled with so many wonderful, remarkable things – gifts, really, from living life, from being part of. An imperial sadness nudges its way in as well, though when I'm mindful I realize it's often like a vampire, needing an invitation. But, not always. Being sad for loss is as real as smiling over butterflies.

This is my third writing today -it's 9:35 am – my everyday Morning Pages followed by my most-of-the-time 'timed writings', these last few weeks clocking at 25:25. And now this post. I've been writing myself out, I know, trying to get to where and when I stray off gratitude and is it me or is it that particular time, and how best to allow the harder stuff to pass while jumping up and going all in on the dance with my blessings.

It does feel like many of my Blog posts since I arrived in Encinitas July 3 have been similar in their content and much of the language employed – there, you might say, are those words again. Found here, again, in what I originally called my "daily weather reports". It's just the way it is, and all I can say is here's me today.

Today, also, is my first day alone with the kids, this absolutely unexpected and truly amazing and enriching opportunity to be part of the lives of a young married couple. My job. I want to keep them safe, that's first, and I want to share the me of me and see if there maybe isn't something in there to enrich their lives as well.

There's grace about.

accouterments

If I were a Catholic, I'd be giving my computer the last rites. As a practicing half-assed Buddhist, I have concluded my computer's 'thusness' is somewhere between life support and scrap heap. Folks have been telling me – my son Cameron most clearly – things get made these days with a corporate eye to giving out sooner than later, means a good computer ought to do its thing like three maybe four years. When they hear mine must be going on eight, well, there's an electric chuckle and a head-shaking in the direction of one clearly not in the know. With the advice it's time to cough up some dough and go get yourself a new one, Pops.

That takes me two places. There's the math-like place where I have convinced myself over the decades (based primarily on fact) that I have the technical skills of a praying mantis (she likely has more) and what about all the wicked important stuff I'll lose in hands thrown-up, make-me-want-to-holler attempts to transfer what's in the antique on which I type this very thing to a shiny new one. I'll fail wildly. There's that. There is also something of a default place as regards money and my history with it (or its invisible twin) and how can I possibly afford to buy a new computer when there's this crazy rent and California gasoline price and me on my Social Security — and all that old noise.

Let me reply – to me.

Regards I ain't the kid from "Ready Player One" and know next to nothing about nothing when it comes to computers – so what? When I think back three and four months to how much of my life I gave away – sold, donated, recycled, shredded, chucked – clearing out it and me from my ex-wife's house, it just had to happen that way. What I told myself at the time was I was about to enter a completely new chapter and so didn't need all the "things" and accouterments and keepsakes from the first 70-plus years. They'd served me enough. Well, it's still true. If I lose photos and files, even if I lose unfinished stories patiently waiting on me for "The End" some five years now, so what? I probably won't lose all that but even if I do, it's like Thoreau said – "Simplify, simplify, simplify."

Then the money thing. Back in 2011, I believe it was March, when I was now legal to "retire" and in a job I pretty much hated, out of the blue late one morning came a phone call from my main man Keith, over in Provincetown, MA, and hearing my thinking Keith immediately told me, "You've got to pray for abundance, Bro. Quit the job. Abundance – it's everywhere. You'll be taken care of. For sure. There's abundance everywhere." That conversation changed my life that day, the next two months when I did resign and retire, and since. The feel-it-and-know-it quality of abundance has remained an intrinsic piece in my life – woven through and through. It was still this morning. In April when I suddenly lost my house and was encouraged somewhat mystically to head down here to San Diego and never mind the "costs", I had some faith. A bunch of it. I'll be taken care of. I believed. And – you've read it here before – folks from my all through my life came back to help me on down this new road. Some gave money. Enough money, even, to buy a new computer.

This morning, after meditating and while drinking coffee and scribbling inspired-from-somewhere ideas into and down onto my notebooks and steno pads – the cheap stuff akin to treasure maps these last 15 weeks – the clear thought came that the very next time my computer crashes (with blue fatal error messages) in the middle of something important to me right then and there – yes, right then and there I'm going on-line (once I can again) and order a new one. Free delivery.

That's decided. Now, when I rented this room here in Encinitas for way more than I had – and hello new job with kids – part of the deal/rent included wifi. It turns out the wifi at this end of the house with amazingly cool and thick walls – wait, let me get all technical here – the wifi sucks when it even works (and it just this second turned off). Meaning if I remain here – and I am wide open to whatever 'the plan' is for me any day I wake up, meaning maybe I won't – but if I do I'm going to have to purchase internet (modem/router/etc.) for my room. Rent my own internet. More money.

And more opportunity to twirl around in the abundance of it all.

pearl of the quarter

I was driving home from one of those early-morning meetings over by the ocean and I was stopped at a boulevard traffic light thinking about Susan – my ex-wife – and how I'd taken a picture of two turtles someone had amazingly and so colorfully painted on a fence near the Pannikin coffee shop and texted it to her because she loves turtles. And how I had not heard a word back, not a "thanks", not anything. And I was thinking that that's her side of the street and I thought to take and send the picture from mine, and mine's the only one I get to do work on, and I suppose I was thinking the no response was cold, and it hurt, and maybe it's enough, now, to let go.

And while stopped at the light, having switched on my CD with the two radio stations I get playing crap songs, on came Steely Dan's "Countdown to Ecstasy", and the cut "Pearl of the Quarter" and out from the radio came this line – "And if you hear from my Louise won't you tell her I love her so." And I got it. Call it an "aha" moment or light slicing through a thickening fog, that was it. I love her this Thursday like I have all these years and I will and I want to, and I only want for her to be happy and feel the joy she creates and deserves, and to live each day in grace. But it seems I'm not allowed to tell her anymore. Even turtles won't do it.

I guess every post I write here is personal – my inside weather – this feels a little more so. If you read this and if you happen to run into or bump into or hear from or have any kind of contact with my ex-wife, won't you please tell her Buddy hopes her days are filled with laughter and joy and grace.

You read that somewhere.

dj me

I had a post mostly written, about half an hour ago, and the internet stopped its web thing and when it came back on a minute later the computer crashed – not even a cursor. Then I turned the computer off and on by hand and the internet came back and now is mostly gone again and the fact is the post I'd written was not very good. So I thought I'd list the songs I played via YouTube on my phone sitting on a rock bench at the end of a long, high-on-a-ridge Friday afternoon walk. The musical choices will do a better job explaining my internal 'weather' today than writer/blogger me.

In order:

"Time Will Tell" – Tower of Power

"Friday I'm in Love" – The Cure

"Destination Unknown" – Missing Persons

"Good Timing" – The Beach Boys

"I'm Gonna Be Strong" – Gene Pitney

"Psychotic Reaction" – The Count Five

and then I headed back here. By the way, I was singing Jan and Dean's "New Girl in School" along the way.

Groundless

Saturday morning I drove a mile to the closest credit union here in Encinitas and opened an account. In order to make the minimum $25 deposit for a new account, I had to use the credit union's atm to withdraw money from my credit union in Portland, Oregon – which is where I have done all my 'banking' business for over a decade, still do my banking business, and will continue to do my banking business. You're a member with them wherever you land in the country.

I did not, therefore, need to open an account at another credit union. So, why'd I do it? I did it because I thought and hoped it would help me feel a little more grounded. The California driver's license and CA tags for the Camry helped me to feel more local. Like a local. As does having an Encinitas address and receiving my mail here. But those realities have not helped me to feel more grounded. Nor actually living here, as I feel very little connection with various housemates or with the idea of "home", which, like that, I always envision finger quotes around when I say the word.

Among many feelings which slowly and surely have been identified by me, within me, and I have talked about the most prominent of them here at Couch Surfing, it has come that I am feeling and experiencing a sense of groundlessness. Not so much disconnectedness, that's been fairly easy for me to feel pretty much anywhere I've been. I'm for the most part an introvert – I've got tests to prove it – and a loner. Most my favorite things to do are alone things. My (ex) wife filled that alone space and introvert human profile a hundred times over. Ten thousand times. So much way more than enough. Then all that sweet emotional energy was gone in an instant and life guided me 1001 miles away. And knowing nearly no one, and having a nearly zero sense of "home", it's been the Pacific Ocean and the "feel" of a beach community doing nearly all the filling of that empty space. And while the endless ocean and surfboards and succulents everywhere are valiant and magnanimous in their efforts, I am left with this feeling of being groundless.

I have reached out and am reaching out to connect with people. I've asked a few people from those "meetings" if they'd like to get a coffee sometime, and one guy actually had me out to his house and it was fun and fulfilling. But he never got around to the coffee and it was in the boonies many, many miles from here, and I told him I'd need to stand on a corner with a can hustling for gas money to come back again, and when I drove away I knew I'd probably not. There are a couple more guys who may be possible, Encinitas guys. Giving time time on them.

Yes, I have a growing familiarity with best driving routes and shortcuts and now four favorite walks and amazingly lush places from which to overlook the ocean. I have a "meeting" place where people recognize me and say hi in genuine welcome. Now I have a California credit union with a whopping balance and it's only a mile away. And I have a job and that is in fact a real ground for me – already people express serious gratitude I've arrived. They mean it. Even the kids seem to like me. And never mind I have twice driven down to Ocean Beach and done things which have become sacred for me over the years, including eating at Hodad's. Though those things solo now.

It's good to have self-awareness. In a recent phone call my friend Kate said we should always be looking at ourselves, as living entities, and working to better ourselves. I have grief – of course. And I have disconnectedness – pretty normal. I have my hopes and dreams too, also normal, and they're big. And my nearly ever-present sense of wonder. That's a gift. I have this Blog, I have my unfinished books staring at me, I have new painting canvases waiting for me to show up with a brush. I even have a brand-new computer in the wind, on the way.

And I have this feeling of groundlessness too. Even with the credit union.

bits….pieces

Squished for time, off in a few minutes for a workday with the kids. Hoping to be a channel of joy.

I went to a movie last night, first time in two, maybe three years. The La Paloma on 101, sort of in the heart of kind of 'downtown' Encinitas. Old-time big theater, one screen. I paid 10 bucks to watch "Roadrunner", a film about Anthony Bourdain. Many moving moments, a few of my lately tears here and there. I came out at dusk with a powerful sense of obligation to use every day I get going forward as creatively and generously and kindly as I can.

Last Friday I went to the Encinitas library hoping to find the "Guardians of the Galaxy" dvd, not there, asked where I could find Kerouac instead, and walked out with Pema Chodron's "When Things Fall Apart". It was exactly what I went there for – I just didn't know it.

Yesterday I finished a walk on the numbered streets by the ocean and sat on a favorite overlook bench and pulled out my phone and just as I did it rang and I saw it identified "Garden State Mike", my old pal Mike from Portland. He'd moved back to his roots a number of years ago, a loss for me, and continued (s) to surf and skateboard and yesterday began his first day as a charter school history teacher in Newark. We'd talked the week before and he said he had an hour commute each way and he was looking forward to it because he had plans to call people. And when that phone call ended with me in my lately tears, I guess he figured he'd make me his first commuting call. And he did. Lucky me.

And the clock has tick-tocked its way to now I get to head over to San Marcos and hopefully spread some joy, maybe sprinkling a little fairy dust on myself in the process.

under the influence of apple pie

At two in the afternoon yesterday, Tuesday, I found myself in a highly-chlorinated swimming pool in an apartment complex in San Marcos, California. About 10 feet away in the water were a young married couple, both with Down syndrome. It was 80 degrees, the sky was bright blue, the water felt real good in a pool never deeper than 5 feet, and out of that bright blue came what was clearly a thought right out of the Talking Heads – "Well, how did I get here?"

I was in a town I'd never heard of two months ago. I was the paid supporter of two young people – hopefully welcoming recipients of my support – who I'd never met a month before. Working for an agency I'd never heard of in all my years traveling to San Diego. Reporting to work to an apartment complex with this lovely if apparently underused pool, with a sweet small gym, and with a parking place I could always expect to find open for me. And with a life I could never, ever have imagined back in mid-April. Nor would have wanted to.

Not really the same as it ever was.

But, I know how technically I got there, and so do you if you are a regular visitor here, because this Blog has masked and served as a travelogue these last four months – first this happened, then this happened, then this one offered a garage and this one offered a room and that angel said of course, I'll take and love your kid. And people sent love and blessings and some cash, people paid too much for paintings, and I sold a bunch of stuff and gave away way more and found myself believing electrically in the "Strange travel suggestions may be dancing lessons from God" Vonnegut hymn.

And on a Tuesday in the middle of the afternoon inland from the ocean I'm with two young people who are so tender toward each other it has already filled my heart with faith and magic – and broke it a little more now that I can't say the same for myself. A receiver and giver of that kind of love.

Apple pie, you wonder? When I reported 15 minutes early for my "shift" the young man saw me come in, got up from the couch and walked to the refrigerator. He opened the door, reached in, and came out with and solemnly handed to me a small food container with the name "Buddy" in marker on a piece of masking tape. Inside, I could see, a slice of heavily-crumbed apple pie. I right there and then felt part of something special, intensely so, the Universe smiling down on me graciously again. I sort of felt loved. Later, after I had made them a distant cousin of omelets for their dinner, and munched on a few pieces of bell pepper and some olives I'd brought in a small cooler, and me being all Keto and everything and almost never eating sugar or bread (Hodad's in Ocean Beach a howling exception), I offered each of them some or even all of it the pie. And they looked at me and said no – "We had our piece. That's your piece."

Since then I've been under that influence of thoughtfulness. And apple pie.

fumbler in the Dell

Not much to say here late on this Thursday afternoon. I did jump into the Pacific and get pushed and pulled around and about some by serious wave action. The salt-water experience was a highlight of the day. This post is being created on my new Dell computer, me finally unplugging the Lenovo which has served me well some eight years and on which I have written all of my eight books and who knows how many love letters to my (ex) wife. And other cool stuff. But crashing with 'fatal error' messages became more and more a way of life and I received good advice to "pull the trigger" and buy the new one – part of my honoring of the golden gifts I've received from the generous among you these last four desperately wild and broken-hearted months. And since I'm writing this, I obviously was able to figure out how to plug it in and turn it on, but pretty much everything else associated with the experience so far has been angst and minor stress and tiny curse words, and all I can do here right after five is keep the faith and believe over time I'll begin to find the webby places and spaces I frequent often, and the tools I've used as a creator. Like I heard at a Red Sox game one time – even a blind squirrel will find an acorn now and then.

There have been other highs and other disappointments in the last 24 hours, blessings received and emotional tests put to. I'm slowly reading Pema Chodron's "When Things Fall Apart" which I went to get at the library last Friday, even though I didn't know that when I walked in. Its relevance to my life today – exactly this time in my life – is shocking. And an amazing gift. And at the library today I dropped off my California ballot to keep Newsom in Sacramento and picked up five art books I'd placed on hold, and a DVD of "The Guardians of the Galaxy."

Pema Chodron writes a lot about "maitri", loving kindness for yourself. And Rocket, one of the Guardians, says "There ain't nobody like me but me." They both feel incredibly relevant here in Encinitas these days, where at least I get to take the good counsel of the Universe and go jump in an ocean.

so noble

I've been talking about the Pema Chodron book "When Things Fall Apart" lately, since I used my library card to borrow it accidently on purpose. Accidently because it was not a dust-mote-sized thought in my mind. On purpose because it was all I went to get. Reading it slowly has brought memories of information I had and used and cared about and don't often bring up to mind except when it's the right time, which now surely is. One of those memories lands on the Four Noble Truths of the Buddha. Here's my Cliff notes version – 1) Life is suffering; 2) This is the way of suffering; 3) There is an end to suffering; 4) This is the way to the end of suffering.

I've read this before and – again – known this before and it's repeatedly noted through the "Fall Apart" book. This – grasping leads to suffering. Grasping for tangible things, for specific situations, grasping for events, grasping for a person. Mostly grasping to have "it" my way. Here's a good, current example for me. I'm often not happy living in the house in which I live. There are things I like, but too often I feel dismissed. I feel, sometimes, like a trespasser. I feel left out. Now, no one has said to me, "You're dismissed." No one has proclaimed, "You're trespassing." But I feel those things, my Spidey senses all alert and on-call . Feeling left out is just them paying attention to me being clear I ain't interested in their playgrounds. So I don't like how it feels to live here and the not liking is the way of suffering. The Second Noble Truth. Life as an "if only".

It's funny. Last Friday I was on what I call the "high" bluff walk and on the last of four back and forths I realized I'd been thinking most of the time about the feelings noted above and some of the time about the ways I could make my room crazy cool and a hotbed of creativity. Some may call this schizophrenia. I know I did, while still on the path, and again at a corner table at the Pannikin coffee shop an hour later. In fact, there I had what would best clinically be described as a fucking meltdown – quietly to and with myself – and kind of flipped out and typed up on my phone a wildly deranged verbiage map of how I needed to be, and mentioned repeatedly I was sick of complaining and whining – absolutely, positively sick of it. Me hearing it and me subjecting others to it. Then I came back to my room and opened the Chodron book and almost immediately read, "In Tibetan there's an interesting word: 'ye tang che'. The 'ye' part means "totally, completely", and the rest of it means "exhausted". Altogether 'ye tang che' means totally tired out. We might say "totally fed up". It describes a feeling of complete hopelessness, of completely giving up hope. This is an important point. This is the beginning of the beginning. Without giving up hope – that there's somewhere better to be, that there's someone better to be – we will never relax with where we are or who we are."

Reading that gave me right then the distinct – and electric – sense of what my former mentor Dick M. was always saying to me – "You're right where you're supposed to be." Relaxing – like, seriously, chill Bro – with where and who I am, on what Pema calls "the middle way", brings me to that Fourth Noble Truth – the way to the end of suffering. I'm nowhere near there today, this Friday. It's a long, long road and it's not likely I'll have the time, in this life, to find myself at the end of it. If there is an end to it. The endless path. The middle way. The just shut the "f" up.

Did I wake up again today? Am I still here? Are there treasure maps all over the place? Am I watched over and cared for by a smiling Universe? Am I capable of at least making my way in baby steps toward that "middle way"? Is there gas in the car, can I get a burrito for dinner, did I jump in the ocean just yesterday, am I offered chances to do special things? Am I loved abundantly by so many? Yes, yes, and endless yes's. So…….

Which "Truth" do I ask to dance an hour from now?

take a bench

Back in January of 2006 when I began a job at Walden House in San Francisco I discovered that the old-time drug rehab-type program there – where I was going to work with kids – continued to make use of slogans as part of the daily routine. Part of the lingo, heard over and over in repetition, find a way into that thick addict persona. Something like that. "Own your own" became one of my favorites, similar like a first cousin to those don't-drink-one-day people saying "Just work your side of the street." I've been saying "Own your own" to myself since. It's good advice. Wicked good.

Another directive, this actually physical in the moment, was "Take the bench." Literally, there were benches placed here and there in the corridors of the large building on Haight Street and when a staff person told one of the young residents to "take the bench" it meant just that – leave here and go there, and while you're there think about what it was that got you there. Why were you sent to the bench? I loved that one too, a super-charged "time out" with big added benefits for potential self-awareness. During my time at 214 Haight I directed lots of the kids to take the bench, and every time I did I knew I was doing them a favor when I said it. In fact I liked that opportunity enough to lead a one-time group on the value of "taking the bench", that group ending with me taking the actual bench I'd brought to the center of the circle of chairs beforehand, picking it up and putting it on my shoulder, and walking away and out the door – my message, in metaphor, there's going to be "a bench" wherever you go. An ever-present opportunity being you decide when you need to take the bench before someone else decides for you. Oh – my pal and mentor Gavin was sitting beside me in that group.

I'm planning to take the bench tonight. This bench is up on the bluff overlook above Moonlight Beach and the Pacific Ocean here in Encinitas. There's a line covering some 50 yards of a lot of benches, each one donated by a family or individual and dedicated to a loved one. My favorite sits forward of the others by a little and is dedicated to a woman named Rebecca. It's not always available, but one of the benches always is, and – I realized this in a flash on my walk early this morning – when I park in the lot or on a nearby street and walk over the tar and the golden-brown wood chips and sit on Rebecca's bench, or Virginia's next to it, or any of the others – I am "taking the bench." Flat-out, crazy time-warped, exactly the same taking the bench. A place of peace. A place of gratitude. A place to send texts to friends, loved ones, a place to make and receive phone calls from those people. To look with wonder and thanks at pelicans floating by, and out to the endless, absolutely endless waves. Always with the opportunity to think about how I'm doing. How am I? Am I in touch with the joy of another day – right here, right now?

So I send myself to the bench every day – I think I've missed one day since I arrived early in July – and it dawned on me this morning it's a bench I picked up in Portland and in Truro and in Lowell and Salem and Wareham and Oakland and everywhere I've landed these 72 plus years and put on my shoulder and brought wherever "here" is today. So I could think awhile about, "How did I get here?"

I'm working with the kids in San Marcos today and when I get back to where "here" is for me now I'm going to make a quick stop and change into my walking shoes and roll the Camry downhill toward the endless ocean and go and find my bench again. Today. Cause that's what we do.

ditch-digging advice

….and on the walk I got to thinking of the two ditch-digger cats who'd roll into the 5:30 gathering of folks hoping to get their lives a bit more together and the one guy every single time would say, "This is the day the Lord hath made, and I will rejoice in it." And big old open-minded me – um, way way younger then – would emotionally/spiritually/foolishly cringe at the word "hath" and so pay as little attention as possible to some kind of religious doctrine-y thing (I felt), and so much for open mindedness. There's a happy ending here, though, from way back when as this was on the east coast of Florida in 1987 and it's me then being able to follow at least some advice, right here it being "keep coming", and this is I'd say a story of the goldenness of repetition, hearing something again and again and again and waiting, likely subconsciously, for the "aha" moment to arrive, cause they do, that's my experience, and maybe it happened one fine day or possibly it leaked in over a few weeks but one of those 5:30 afternoons in a folding-chair seat my editing mind left the troubling word mentioned above and lingered, instead, on the rejoicing in the day part of it.

See, told you it had a happy ending, as since then I have had that wisdom that I can rejoice in a day I am given, haven't always remembered, but more than not as time has passed, and I don't need to tell you (again) how blessed I am to still just be here – I'm still here!!! – I got to wake up again today and this is the day the Universe has sent me and very early on, my 6:15 heading-out walk, I happened to look up and see the moon hanging in the mostly clear sky and I did the walk I do every morning here in Encinitas and thought about those two guys and the kindest advice of all to rejoice in the blessing of a newly arrived day, and I actually twirled in celebration, a complete 360, crossing the then-empty boulevard and continued on my walk and saw some cool stuff and waved at the same people I see early every morning, a couple of Mexicans and a crazy and wildly friendly walking lady dressed in flowing black, and here I am, my life so different and able to feel my feelings more keenly, and aware that I get nudged and sometimes shoved toward the next spot of right where I'm supposed to be, and for me this morning that was out early looking at the moon and thinking of something I heard long ago.

And these days it's my welcome companion, always with me even when I forget to look, and mostly I don't forget to look, and I sat down here at the keyboard early because this is another work with the San Marcos kids day and I have to call the County at 9 about senior benefit business and my great pal and life partner Keith, now in Greenwich

Village, sent me a bag of acrylic paints and lovingly-used brushes which arrived in the mail yesterday – abundance – and it felt exactly right being with the kids yesterday and then back with mostly green lights (so whimsical) and over to the ocean and, yeah, taking a bench and aware of this is me here now, and then a brief walk and the rest of the night was interesting and I spontaneously bought something on-line which I'll talk about, I bet, sometime soon, and suit up and show up, they said, and keep on keeping on, kid, life advised me in the sixties, and here in Southern California in 2021 I'm doing the best I can and sometimes I forget and become a whiner and it's stupid and I'm trying for more awareness and for sure I'm mostly remembering to "rejoice in it", and that's about it.

sleepwalk

While out with the large push broom sweeping clean the long driveway here early this morning the idea of sleep-walking through life drifted into my mind. I guess because I realized I had to give full attention, in this case visual, to what I was doing. Otherwise, the broom would whimsically skip over some of the dropped needles from the tall Torrey Pine out front, or the brush would hold as if in deep love certain needles and gently drop them back behind where I was sweeping. No, serious attention is required sweeping this driveway, sleepwalking will not do.

Of course, since I sort of measure my life in the music of all the times I've been fortunate enough to live through so far up 'til this morning, the song "Sleepwalk" by Santo and Johnny came to mind. I'd quote you a few lyrics except there aren't any. One of those fine opportunities to be quiet and listen. Maybe you remember the song, if you were lucky enough to live through the 50's and 60's and are still with us. Let me see if I can imbed a link here:

I know this – I've been talking way too much. Miss a bunch of the music that way. Time's too precious. I woke up again. I'm still here. I cleared the driveway of gravity's work and a cool tree renewing itself. And thought of a childhood song and came back to my room and played it and it made me happy and going forward here on an already-interesting Wednesday, the best of me will be listening. And paying the best wide-awake attention I've got today.

Howling

I lick my arm and it tastes like salt. I'm typing this in a damp bathing suit. These are good things. I've never used sunscreen, ever, and I'm brown as a Torey pine trunk and I have my first Doctor's appointment in forever, and the first one down here in SoCal, tomorrow morning, and I guess I'll begin to find out how things are, including all the funny things my skin's been saying.

The other night, impulsively in the moment, though I'd been considering it for a couple of days, I bought a boogie board. Actually, the brand I wanted after doing some research those 'considering days', came in a two-pack, with way cool colors, and in the moment I hit "buy now", and the package came today. I'm all salty and further reddened and water in my ears and up my nose because I was out there in the ocean at Moonlight Beach an hour ago, boogie-ing my little butt as best as a 72-year old rookie could. This rookie, anyway. It's been a dream of mine my whole life to surf and this felt like a little step down the watery path of dreams. Plus, for years at Ocean Beach with my wife I watched seven- and eight-year old's go flying past me on their boards, their faces lit up with joy and glee and push-it-real-good magic. And I wanted some of that and the clock ticks on, so I hit the "buy it" button and they came today and now ain't no one can say I ain't a boogie boarding fool.

Ironically, it was not my first time on a boogie board. Yesterday, after coffee with my new pal Anthony, I drove to the beach and found a space in the lot – I had my bathing suit on under my cargo shorts – and got out in the water and thanked the Great Spirit that this broken-hearted cat can find mystical solace in the Pacific Ocean. And right there was this couple with their two kids and they were all doing it and the parents caught a couple of rides at the cusp of pretty big breaking waves and shot right past me, and after the second time I went over and said I'm 72 and I've never done it but I have boards on order and time flies and I need to do it, so it was great seeing you have such fun. And about 10 seconds later the dad called out "hey" and he had two boards and said his wife was finished for the day and did I want to give it a try. Right now, this second, right in front of me as I type this, is a piece of paper with the Goethe saying, "Be bold and mighty forces will come to your aid" which I've been holding onto since the middle of April. Here was more proof, and I said thank you so much and tried it four times and the last time I got a pretty good ride. I know I didn't have that childhood gleam of amazement I've seen so often, but it was great.

And today I was out there quite a while and there were lots of waves, endlessly one right after another, and I screwed up and left too early and left too late and one time got my ass kicked big time. Yet there were those four or five times I went flying up on top of the Pacific, like a flying fish, and the best ride of all took me all the way from pretty far out to right up on the beach.

All I can do is say thank you to the Universe for its ongoing generosity and kindness for a damaged kid, me with a touch of boldness thrown in as spice, and so sure that grace is a thing. Oh yeah, on two of those wave-energized rides through the shallow ocean, I was out there howling in delight. I heard me.

I see you

This has been a day – already by 1:08 – with many challenges, some disappointments, and, of course, the never-ending-ness of wonders.

I believe I will close out this week of posts with simply this:

I see you Friday.

Liquids

Friday I had my first medical appointment in something like forever, down in Carmel Valley with a doctor from South Africa who I selected as my primary because I thought she'd have a cool accent – which she did, more of an echo like she'd lived away from the Cape of Good Hope awhile now. Mostly pronounced me medically okay, she said to my question the blotches appearing under my skin on my forearms were the result of – um – old age and banging my arms and capillaries breaking under the skin, and this was the 2021 way of bruising for you she explained. I said I don't remember banging my arms all those times and she said you did, it doesn't take much with your decades, more gently than that, and I went home and was at this keyboard typing and I felt something on my left arm and looked down and one of those blotches had torn through the skin and I was bleeding and it figures stuff happens right after the appointment. And Gavin, later, said take a picture and send it to her and I did take the pic, but it remains anonymous in my phone.

I took it after I'd gone boogie boarding at Moonlight Beach for the third straight day and I was leaking blood on my way out and walking around hoping for the bathing suit to dry. I tell you this as a prelude to the real story which is Saturday I drove down to Ocean Beach in San Diego and walked the Sunset Cliffs along with an amazingly resonating phone call from my long-time mentor Mark in Florida, and then back to where I'd parked and slipped out of my shorts to the bathing suit already on and for the first time carried a boogie board a long way to a beach and went in the rather chilly water where 10 years ago I had first seen children fly by with looks of amazement and thrill, which I wanted, and I managed to stay in 15-20 minutes and boogied (watery-like) a bunch of times and about four really cool rides and one was wicked – the ocean energetic and fired up and me flung over and through like a frisbee skimmed on water back and forth between Ariel and her dad. Of course, I was properly band-aid-ed and forget about the cut and when I got my stuff and found a bench to clean my feet I noticed the band-aid dangling and blood dripping again and so I got myself together (relatively) and walked out across the street and stuck my head in the open door of a surf shop called "The Shed" and asked would they by any chance have a band-aid? And the manager said let me look and they (he and helper) didn't but ended up wrapping gauze with stretchy material and taping it on – so cool – and I said I had no money but I'd be back sometime when I did and they said forget it, glad to help, and I walked backed to my car, carrying my board almost like (big stretch here) a surfer (wheeee) and put my shorts on and went back and walked the famous pier which I've loved more than a decade now and then went back to The Shed and bought a tank-top with their logo and a "Surfer's Journal" and said words to the effect of what goes around comes around, and they gave me some free decals. Then I walked around the corner to eat my fun Keto-busting, famous-chocolate-shake-late-lunch at Hodad's – another big time sacred space – and nothing short of a near-miracle had me fourth in line, instead of the usual around the corner, and the three girls in front of me were called in just as I stepped behind them, making me first like on the immediate level, and I had a yummy and sugary lunch and left and took a bunch of pics of painted murals on walls all around and then slowly walked back, and I said out loud, "I hate leaving Ocean Beach", cause I did.

So maybe this is a story about old age, or the strange paths of sharing time with a soulmate who shows you the best stuff and then says adios and the best stuff is still waiting – not exactly the same but different in an okay suit up, show up way. Maybe it's about good thing there's no vampires in my life (I'm aware of), or of having a new doctor who talks with a cool voice and says you will do what I tell you and I said yeah and so started taking Vitamin D Sunday, but said no to a pneumonia vaccination because the last time I had one I was sick like I had it for three days and she said pneumonia vaccinations don't get you sick and I said "Oh yeah?" Or maybe this story is about a 72.5-year-old gypsy-like character who never forgets how blessed he is even when passing through periods of pitiable whining.

And remembering also heard on the day of the divorce word -- "Be bold and mighty forces will come to your aid." Like asking for a band-aid in a surf shop, and here I am boogie boarding up and down the SoCal coast and hopefully it's about the blessing of hanging onto childlike wonder, and even that kind of children's faith, another day. Maybe, come to think of it, it's just about waking up and getting up – that gift – once more.

Let's do it again

Couch Surfing at 70 today is reconnoitering – pondering the reality testing of a worm-hole-like shuttle through time back to an alternative existence at age 15 – see me here, mellow beach bum.

This is work in progress. To be shared as revealed.

More tomorrow.

down in Doheny

Yesterday I was able to leave my work shift with the San Marcos kids early because they are off to an eight-day vacation with one of the sets of parents this morning, picked up early to avoid traffic jams where possible. Means I rolled out just before three and cruised back to Encinitas, a stop at Trader Joe's and then back to my room for some grocery finagling and a change into a bathing suit under my shorts. Then a glide mostly downhill to the Moonlight Beach parking lot for a hopefully big fun time and with necessary greater in-the-moment consciousness out there in the Pacific on my boogie board.

We've had a fair amount of rain these last few days, darned unusual for these parts in August, and more cloudy skies as a result, so when I arrived at 4pm there was no one in the water. I could see a few people farther down toward the cliffs on the Oceanside side, but not a single soul out from the main beach. That got me wondering and when I walked down, I saw a sign warning about rip tides and swim to the side out of them, so I went to the lifeguard station and asked if there were wicked bad rip tides today and he said no. I asked if that sign's been there all summer and he said yes – yet another example of being intentional with mindfulness because left to my casual self – it's easy to miss stuff. I asked had the water temp dropped and he said not really – people just don't go in the ocean so much when it's cloudy. I said thanks, and being on a mission I did my clothes-and-shoes thing and went into the water, now with a few others. I managed to catch some good rush-along rides and had more misses. Leaving too early or too late, and as the ocean passes by I believe I hear it laughing. It's good to be a source of laughter on the planet. I make note I missed that chance and wait for another. In terms of riding waves and white water, there will be another.

This is a new life for me and maybe it was in the water or back on the beach or on one of the top-of-the-bluff benches which have become sacred places for me, anyway, the idea came that I'm becoming something of a beach bum and – wait, it was while I was at the kids house writing some fly-into-my-head thoughts, yeah it was there, the thought came I'm being sent back in time, way back, to when I was a kid in a town by Cape Cod singing Beach Boys songs on the small front lawn and dreaming about California and what a surfing life would be like. But like back then and through much of my life, dreaming didn't translate into doing. Now, these days – with an assist from a plan not of my choosing — dreaming and doing are walking closer together. Yes, I was at the kids' table and had a vision of me being something of a beach bum – like that 60's song said – "We all live for the sun." – and living a life where I work just enough to barely make the rent, using some savings too, and buy a few groceries, because the important thing is being over there by the ocean, walking, looking, mesmerized, or better yet in the ocean, allowing the great gift of salt water to buoy me up and take me for a ride.

And if I had hair maybe it would bleach lighter, and in fact my skin has that summery look, and I did buy two new bathing suits to go with the one I drove down with from Portland because can't be putting on a wet one under my shorts. And now I have two towels in the trunk of the Camry and the boogie board there as well, and a plastic bag to keep my keys in which are tucked in one of my running shoes and hopefully left alone on the sand until I get back out and go rinse my feet and my sunny-side self.

All this is just me daydreaming here on the keyboard, seeing how it is now, and it's likely that in the beach bum live-for-the-sun remembrances all those cats had friends and buddies and pals to hang with and surf with and goof with and I do not have that yet. But you never know. This life feels right now – work enough to stay afloat (ha-ha) and write because that's what I do, and walk a lot because that's what I do too, and go to Pannikin and drink coffee and read and scribble because there's always that, and now become like that Surfer Joe guy from the song, not exactly, this little close-to-the-shore-move-with-the-ocean's-energy experience smaller. The point is it feels like a time-travel back to an entirely different me at age 15 and traveling down a different path, and I'm not 15 and the big clock tick-tocks quicker now, and the San Marcos kids have gone and I have 12 days without that chance to be a channel of joy and delight and possibility and help pay the rent.

So, what will I do with any day I'm lucky enough just to wake up again? You can find out by coming over to the beachside and checking me out. I'll be there.

dancing in the moonlight

Someone hit my car in the Moonlight Beach parking lot while I was boogie boarding this afternoon. It was my best day of boogie boarding yet, my sixth time out with my board, I caught the most waves and missed the fewest, better ratio of success than previous days. Also, a couple of very fast rushes through and over the ocean. I saw a couple of different people look at me with something that maybe stood for appreciation. That felt cool.

Then I got to my Camry up above in the lot, and the left rear bumper and some of the left rear quarter had clearly been hit by another car, scrapes and paint off in a couple of spots, black lines and a circle of worse than anywhere else. Cosmetic – but, still. No note, no eyewitnesses, no way for justice if something like that merits justice. I flashed on me and my black 2001 Taurus pulling out of the lot behind the 214 Walden House boys' facility and scraping the right rear bumper and quarter, 15 years ago, and somehow my mind took me to a place where there was some kind of weird balance.

I know.

I also went for a walk after discovering the bring-down from best yet boarding and on the way back I flashed on "The Fast Times at Ridgemont High" character Spicoli – who I'm identifying with a lot these days, sans the smoking dope – and a conversation he might have with a friend, where the friend says, "Someone hit my car, man", and Spicoli says, 'Yeah, but there's a war in Bosnia, Bro. Which is worse?" That made me feel better too.

So, with practice and repetition I'm a better boogie boarder this Thursday than I was last Thursday. Not a lot, but better. And my car is a little worse for wear this Thursday than it was last Thursday. Not a lot worse, but not quite the visual pleasure of a couple hours earlier.

On the way down to the beach I ran into my new pal Brad who was cruising in his motorized wheel chair and I yelled his name and he swung around and we talked water temp and southerly swells and truly painful breakups from one you love. Then he motored over to his van and I went boogie boarding and someone scraped along my car with their car, and all of it made me feel at one with my 2006 piss-poor cornering at Walden House self, and at one with Spicoli too. I don't eat much pizza anymore, like him, and I haven't smoked dope since Reagan's first. But I am just a bit more of a "middle way" laid-back beach bum these days.

Life being lifey.

rings and things

I did not have a story for the Blog for the final weekday of this week until I went to the beach.

I was involved in stay-at-my-room stuff until about 12:30 when I drove over beachside and went for a walk and for a coffee and reading at Pannikin. Then I drove to the Moonlight parking lot and walked down, boogie board under my arm, the sky clouded over and the air cooler, running into my friend Brad in his motorized chair, on the phone with his sweetie, who, he yelled out, said to say hello to me. Then I walked onto the beach – right or left – went left, set the board down and my towel down, took off my running shoes and socks and hid my keys in the sock stuffed into one of the shoes, took off my tank top, and got up to go boogie-ing.

It was then I noticed a woman directly in front of me moving her hands slowly through the sand, and a guy beyond her to her right doing the same. "Did you lose something?" I asked, and she said yes, his wedding ring. I experienced a wave of sadness. I asked if I could help look and I moved my feet and my hands, standing up and kneeling down, for about 15 minutes before an idea came to me, and it was one of those "right where I'm supposed to be" times. Surely. I've never taken off my wedding ring these last approaching five months, my only jewelry I'd say to myself, I like the way it feels when I twirl it with my thumb I'd say to myself, it just shouldn't come off I say to myself. But I looked at the guy and said, "Do you want to try this one on? I'm not being weird, my wife divorced me four months ago and I haven't been able to take it off." And he said "Okay."

He tried it and said it fit pretty good and what felt like the enormity of giving away my wedding ring – been on that finger 11 and a half years – had me wonder aloud if maybe he'd consider borrowing it until he came across another he knew was the one for him, and they could mail mine back to me. His name is Alex and his wife's name is Amy, they're in Encinitas for a Saturday wedding and couldn't not come to the beach, she said. They said okay, and I gave Amy my info, which she put in her phone. I looked some more for his ring and then walked out into the surf, but the fact is my boogie-ing mostly sucked today, I was not all "there" for it, and after a short time I came out and spent another 10 minutes looking for Alex's ring. No dice. They thanked me again and I walked off the beach and found myself in tears for I think all the right reasons. Mostly for feeling so alive these days, even when being alive aches like crazy. On the way up to rinse the board and my feet I ran into Brad again and told him and cried a little more, and I said a month or so ago, looking for a pair of socks in the travel bag on the floor by my bed, I thought I saw a wedding ring – it would be my wife's ring and she would have thrown it in there without me knowing and that broke my heart some more when I saw it, but I was going to go back now and look for it. And Brad said don't put on your wife's wedding ring.

But I knew I would if I found it, and I'm looking at it on my ring finger now. It's my new jewelry. My thumb is already playing with it. If the other shows up one of these days from Arizona, where Amy and Alex live, I'll take this one off and put it back in the bag and put mine back on.

I woke up today, this Friday, feeling sad. I still do. I also feel useful, in a help the planet along way. My old running buddy Frenchie, from back in my early 80's Somerville days, always use to say, "I don't know nothing about nothing." Some days I really dig that."

with this ring – Part 2

If you read the Blog Friday you saw the tale of the gifted wedding ring. Here now, this Labor Day, come three updates:

One – I incorrectly identified the young couple from Arizona as Amy and Alex. It's Abby and Alex. I don't like making factual errors when I write anywhere – unless my pal Milky Dent and I are just making stuff up – and especially not in this Blog. I apologize to Abby and Alex, and to my readers.

Two – In fact, as I reported, I did find my ex-wife's ring in the bottom of my travel bag and I did put it on and it did feel good there on my ring finger – twirlable, comfortable, lovable even. But only for a while. By bedtime that night I had taken it off my finger and placed it on the table next to the computer. When I woke Saturday I took the ring and put it back in the bottom of my bag. It's not mine, and that's where that ring belongs. So I have been ring-less since Saturday morning, and I cannot say how many times I had a few seconds of panic in the ocean both Saturday and Sunday that my ring had slipped off into the water. A part of me no longer there.

But….

Three – Here's a happy ending. I ran into the lifeguard, my friend Brad, in his motorized chair Sunday morning and the first thing he asked was if I'd got my ring back. I held up my empty hand and said no, why? He said someone with a metal detector had showed up and discovered Alex's ring and turned it in. I texted Abby after a bit and told her what I'd heard, and a few minutes later Abby texted me back and said, yes, it was true, and Alex had his wedding ring. I'm sure wearing it right then. And they were in the car on the way back to Arizona, she wrote, and when they get back they're going to put mine in the mail and send it back to me.

I guess I'll say where it belongs – my wedding ring on my left-hand ring finger – and any reader can decide for themselves what they think about that. Crazy to still wear it? Delusional? Childish? Such a romantic?

Boy, I hope all of those are true. And the Platters song you had to pass by to get to the lingo here today. It's always been a favorite of mine, and what it expresses is as real for me today, sitting here at the keyboard, as it was any time during the last 11-plus years.

How can me still loving someone so special be anything but right?

ride my see saw

It's Tuesday afternoon and a while ago I introduced myself to a guy I've spoken with a few times now. He's waiting on a license to operate a concession at Moonlight Beach and he rents boogie boards and ocean devices and sells t-shirts and accessories and all that touristy stuff and we've spoken a few times, and today I said what's your first name and he said Justin and I told him mine was Buddy and we shook and I went up to sit on one of the sacred benches overlooking the ocean and let my bathing suit dry out, then put the board and towel and t-shirt back in the Camry, parked out on the street, and went for a further-drying walk. And on the way back I told myself to please remember that cat's name, Justin, and I thought of the Moddy Blues because I'm pretty sure there was a guy named Justin in that group.

So, Tuesday afternoon and Justin and The Moody Blues and why wouldn't I think of all that. The owner of the home in which I rent a room for crazy money and get my own bathroom sometimes and use of the kitchen when I sneak in and out like a mischievous cat, she's my landlady you might say and she is throwing a birthday party for herself tomorrow night. An annual tradition I understand, and she has warned me there will be some 50 people in attendance and she has warned me the partying will carry on until 11 or so, and I have said I hope everyone has a great time and it's wonderful so many people are coming to your party – some from Brazil and some from Mexico by the way – and the six people living here now (normally two) who have never used an alias of Milky Dent all know I'm not coming or maybe I'll come for a few minutes, which I've said I will so as not to be entirely anti-social, and I don't think they give a rat's ass in hell that I don't drink and do drugs anymore than I don't give a rat's ass in hell if they do, or smoke banana peels or shoot up green tea mixed with belladonna. But the pre-party organizing and festivities have me acting like the good kid we heard about in the old days – not seen and not heard.

Oh, warning me that the party is going to go on all the way until 11 is akin to telling me everyone's going to get really crazy and eat three M & M's each, maybe even four, you believe it!! In other words – rookies.

I saw and introduced myself to Justin up from the ocean's edge, and I'd been out in the water quite a while, sunny and warm today like it hasn't been so much lately, and the big waves of the weekend lingered and I caught some massively giddy-up rides, and had my cute and slightly withered butt kicked dramatically about three times also. And while I was up near the outdoor showers wiping sand off my feet some guy came by on a bike and asked if I had good rides and I said yeah and then he told me why I was doing things improperly, lack of righteous equipment he explained – and he knew a bunch of people who had broken their necks doing what I'd just been doing. So I figured I would tell him that I knew a bunch of people who had been struck by lightning and electrocuted doing what he was doing – riding a bike. But quite recently I have taken a heavy vow of 100% honesty so I said thanks for sharing and went back to the wet sand between my toes.

And I'd been on a long sweaty walk before my boogie boarding fantasia and while on it I thought about big loneliness, which I feel, and I thought about how many parking spaces there were everywhere the day after Labor Day – so great. And the fact is I'm more unhappy living in my expensive room than I am happy, even when I'm full-on a warrior for the middle way. And I am beyond amazed that I am nearly a certified beach bum at age 72.5, meaning I live in a beach-side town and do ocean things and bow daily to the never-ending-ness of all the beauty and majesty, and Justin told me there'd be days like today all the way through October and the water would stay mostly warm, and then I drove home to my room and people were in the meow kitchen making stuff for tomorrow and I hung my towel and suit out to dry in the Encinitas sunshine and came to the keyboard.

And of course the song "Ride My See Saw" had come into my mind earlier. Why not. My life has that see saw up and down-ness to it now, which my warrior mind controls a lot of but not entirely – not yet. And the Moody Blues sang it.

don't know mind

I woke this morning with a don't know mind. I like that, I like being in that mind. It's a pathway to staying in the moment. Like, what will you do if you find a dead mouse on the concrete path to your favorite ocean viewpoint? I don't know. What will you do if current housemates lobby you incessantly to attend tonight's 'wild' party? I don't know. Where will you be living Thanksgiving day? I don't know. Will you become a boogie boarding legend, starting so late in life and all that? I don't know. Will you fall in love again? I don't know. If the internet fails? I don't know.

I don't know leaves me with nothing but the moment. It's a close cousin to another favorite – Now what? That's a question I've asked myself a whole bunch over the years. It's another right here, right now doorway – Now what?

Allen Ginsberg calls what showed up in meditation the "Surprise Mind." Another goodie.

Being a devoted warrior for the middle way, being in this very moment – open to it, listening to it, surprised by it, moving with it – is to be on the path. At least how I see it today. And fortunately, this Wednesday, I woke up (by itself such a blessing) with a don't know mind.

Who knows what tomorrow will bring?

I don't.

twice blessed

Once:

I was sitting in Pannikin thinking my Blog post today would be only three or four of five words.

Already I'm wrong.

But, not by much.

Twice:

White bougainvillea falling, drifting to the ground. Like snowflakes.

Here in Encinitas in the summer.

Amazed at their own beauty.

joe friday

Another Friday, me lucky enough to still be here – above ground, on the planet – and I'm back at Moonlight Beach with my boogie board. Set my towel down pretty much in the same place I did last Friday, where you may remember I came upon a young couple running their fingers through the fine Moonlight sand, in search of the lost wedding ring. The story goes I joined in the search, having lost my marriage and feeling some immediate sorrowful connection, and all our sandy search failing to find Alex's ring, I had the feeling he was supposed to have mine, still there on my wedding finger. I offered and he said yes. And later a metal detector dude came along after the fact and found it and turned it in and Alex got his ring back – thank you to the Gods who oversee our sea sides – and we connected by text Sunday and Abby said they'd put mine in the mail back in

Arizona, and I looked in the Friday mailbox today and it still has not arrived. And I guess it will arrive or it won't. And my lonely finger and the thumb that plays with its empty space will accommodate to this be-here-now dance of life.

Last Friday was cloudy and a bit chilly. Today is gloriously sunny and warm, and I was out there having a pretty good time and trying to employ some turning and stopping lessons I've watched on YouTube the last few days. And I ran into the same Brad character I did twice last Friday. There was more kind and caring talk. Without any tears from me.

That's about it. Joe Friday popped into my mind while in search of a title, and though there's no connection to the above report I can see, I went with it. That choice made me think of the song "Killer Joe", which I just played on You Tube, and it turns out that song was recorded by a group named "The Rocky Fellers." Who knew?

Stay safe out there.

coming back to you

My wedding ring came back to me in the mail this morning. From Arizona. From Abby and Alex.

There was a note.

"Dear Buddy – Thank you so much for all of your help at Moonlight Beach. Of all the people who passed by, you were the only one to help us look for Alex's ring and you went above and beyond. It was so very kind of you to let us borrow your ring. We will never forget your generosity and think of you each time we go back to Encinitas. Keep in touch.

Love, Abby and Alex S"

pretty this and that

Bruce Springsteen has a line in one of his songs which goes, "Man the dope is that there's still hope." I've always dug that.

Pema Chodron, Buddhist nun, suggests giving up hope is part of the pathway to end suffering. This is it – right here, right now. Hoping is wishing and wishing is grasping and grasping is very clearly a pathway to suffering. I get it.

It's Tuesday. I'm soon off to work with a couple of pretty remarkable young people. I'm planning to bring the best me to share. Like, as a channel. Sure hope I do.

I'm a writer and an artist. Not too much writing and very little art-ing these days. Dreams of more, to be sure, which I guess may be another word for you know what.

I'm pretty much me – right here and right now – though, which is pretty good

a great wind

Regards today, I am mostly wordless.

A great wind has blown me across the sky.

a Thursday report

I went into the water today. I'd missed out the last three days, working with the kids in San Marcos Monday and

Tuesday, then understanding there were strong rip currents from big swells rolling into the San Diego beaches. Yesterday I brought my board to the ocean but left it on the sand and waded out to about shin high, standing there like that maybe 20 minutes, staring out at waves forming far from shore and heading in, folding over – some with little barrels like you see in movies (Lindsey Lohan, the end of "Soul Surfer"). I experienced something between a mesmerized state and so consciously filled with gratitude – the way I imagine people feel in church, or an art museum, or maybe being interviewed on "American Bandstand". You remember those kids – "I gave that wave a 75. You could dance to it."

Today I ran into Brad on the way down to the beach. He works for the city as a life guard, and this includes him being in a motorized wheel chair. We talked about the water and he said he'd been at it – a life at the water's edge – so long he could come pretty close to guessing the exact temperature of the water from the feel of the wind blowing in. He said to me, don't worry, I wouldn't chicken out from cold or leftover rip current, I'd get wet.

And I did. My rides were mediocre, the waves folding over farther out than my comfort limit, so mostly white water slides and glides. I'm happy I live near the ocean again, who knows know how long I will, and I'm living a fantasy as sort of beach bum, scraggly struggling writer, gypsy child, and worshiper of coffee – especially in to-go cups at Pannikin.

This has been a Thursday report of my personal milieu in Encinitas.

My heart come all undone

Internet's been off in my room most of the day – this will be quick.

I came up from the beach and a sweet boogie boarding session to the Moonlight parking lot, which was closed to parking so as to provide space for a show of restored and absolutely knock-out beautiful woodies. You know, station wagon shaped-vehicles with wood side paneling. You know – "In my woody I will take you everywhere I go."

One of my three all-time favorite songs – "Surfer Girl" – and favorite lines. And there I was, in a collective of wood-paneled beauties.

The idea hung with me. Take your sweetie and go for a ride. Drive anywhere, just that image, lovers in a car cruising together. Out for a ride. One of life's gifts.

If you have a sweetie, treat yourself right. Get in the car. Wood on the side or not.

I would. Everywhere I go.

water's edge

Overheard in Edgewater, Florida circa 1986: "This is the day the Lord hath made, and I will rejoice in it."

Took me a while to get past "hath".

Rejoicing in it has become a way of life.

Monday.

from the Cyrkle

"I should have known you'd bid me farewell
There's a lesson to be learned from this and I learned it very well.

Now I know you're not the only starfish in the sea.
If I never hear your name again, it's all the same to me…
And I think it's gonna be all right
Yeah, the worst is over now,
The mornin' sun is shinin' like a red rubber ball."

Seriously??

I kind of like "Turn Down Day" much better. Like this Tuesday.

"Nothing on my mind…."

no brakes

Oh, sort of moaner, on the edge of moaning, but more than enough in the moment consciousness of my blessings, even being here to note the things which are less than splendid in my life. What a gift, Pema would say. Wow – the big wide-open chance for wisdom mind. Man, I'm loopy this morning. Oh, how the sundowns the last two nights have blessed my soul, and here's a thought, it might make a whole bunch of sense to bring myself to the Moonlight bench and a D Street railing every single night, beginning two nights ago and forward with any day I'm given. I'm flush with gas money, even a brand-new offer of funding and a wicked big check. And when I'm there, I'm not here – duh. I do need to refrain from massive chocolate intake, like last night – my bad – otherwise, are you kidding me?

Bumming by the ocean, glad tidings for my fellow lookers and surf cats. Because I don't know if I'll have the same opportunity a month from now. I just don't, and it's entirely possible I won't.

So, Brah, hie thee to the beachside every night. So, maybe I'll drop out eight or nine words from the last page for the Blog. I do feel that at some hour today I could sit at the keyboard and just rave on. But, I'd worry about the semblance or interpretation of whining and moaning and, honestly, I don't know if I'm a good enough writer today to write it so that (interpretation) is not an option – seeing it that way. But, who knows? I guess when I show up to the keyboard I'll find out. That saying – I write so I can see what I'm thinking – I guess the thing with the ants is take it as it comes – now this – and stop swearing and any sorry-ness for myself – keep aiming toward, "What a present" – and I'll say, I see you ants and I am sorry and then send as many as I can to their heaven so I can feel okay putting my (bare) feet on the floor. Like I had the thought while walking –

signed up to the boot camp, so cool, with my birth certificate chuckling, and maybe all of what feels hard are simply chuckles from the Universe – "Boy, do we have a live one here" – and perhaps it goes without saying, "How'd this guy get so lucky?" Far out, easy-going, channeling, joy job. Fucking boogie boarding. Dig that older guy flying over the water, Holmes, and my cool car, and some wondrous walking, and, oh, so much abundance and a few people who genuinely dig me, and now, geez, the oncoming for a brand-new adventure – look how many (adventures) this kid gets – and three days away from another Keto-breaking celebration, you deserve it, kid, wildly joyous meal at Hodad's. So much. So unendingly blessed. And, Pema's telling me, blessed some more with the unknown and open to being scared, or furious, or something else. Big mind. Here right now. Nowhere's else to be, Brah. And I thought the post would be eight or nine words.

today's Thursday weather

The me of me today:

I have given notice to move from the room I am renting, to be out by October 22. As was the case some five and a half months ago – when my then-wife Susan asked me for a divorce and said I needed to move out – I face directly ahead the reality of no known address.

I have made this decision for the following reasons: (a) I pay an exorbitant amount of rent for a room in which the internet/wifi works and doesn't work whimsically. It has been off much of the last three days, many days of the two and a half months I've lived here. (b) The room I rent is periodically taken over by ants. Lone lines of endless ants, which have been everywhere in my room. The last four days by my bed. The first thing I do nearly every day – before I get on my knees to ask for help and to have a grateful heart, before I sit in meditation – is turn on the flashlight on my phone and slowly walk through the room to see if there will be any lines of ants on which I will be kneeling or sitting. (c) The amount of alcohol and 420 use in the house, and often directly in front of me, has simply become too much. I'm reminded by friends of the saying, "You hang around in a barbershop long enough, you're going to get a haircut."

Today's weather includes not being able to post for a room on Craigslist, which is how I found this one. Every post I try to put up is immediately 'flagged' and removed. This could be the Universe detouring me to a more interesting route of inquiry and personal advocacy. Or someone out to get me. I don't know.

I have received a notice from the California DMV that my newly achieved and paid-for vehicle registration will be suspended October 8. For lack of insurance. As I have insurance, and have pointed it out including during the registration process, I've learned this week my 'Oregon' insurance doesn't count (Nation-wide company).

I'm back on cholesterol medication.

This is some of today's weather, much of it clearly needing my right-away and ongoing focused attention. Also part of my weather today is the wonderful opportunity I'm getting to be of service with the San Marcos kids. The fact I've had the chance to learn how to boogie through the ocean on a board. A fabulous beach-bum existence. The weather is stunningly beautiful. I have met a few people who pretty clearly like and respect me.

Also, I remain heart-broken and here-and-there weepy with the loss of my marriage and no longer getting to be with my best friend, my soulmate. I'm so grateful I got my wedding ring back. It matters to me.

So – If any of this sounds like I'm whining and complaining to you, then I have not written well, I haven't made myself clear. Back on January 22nd of this year, a Friday, I made a vow that I would post daily, Monday through Friday, in this 'Couch Surfing' Blog. I have not missed one day. I said on that Friday my posts would be a report, for any particular day, of how I was feeling on the inside, and what was going on in my life – both inside and out. That is all today's post is. These are many of the facts I woke to this Thursday. Now it's time for breakfast.

P.S. – I would much prefer not being told I'm an idiot (asshole) for giving notice to leave where I live without having another place to go. Like, how many times do you get to roll those dice? If, however, you can't help yourself and just are bursting to call me a complete moron, this will be my default response to you – and to anyone else going forward:

c i g f d

(Cause I'm gonna fucking drink).

yes, in Virginia, there is a Santa Clause

Today would have been my wedding anniversary. Maybe it still is. I've been thinking about it, but haven't come to any decision. I suppose if you stop believing in Santa Clause, December 25th is still Christmas. So, I guess I think it's more likely that it remains my anniversary. I guess.

I sent my ex-wife a small smiley face emoji thing early, actually it was exactly 6:59 this morning. Not one of those big grinning faces, nah, just a small smile. It felt like a look of kindness to me and it felt like a kindness to send it. I didn't expect to hear back – she's not built that way anymore – and I didn't. My side of the street. I get to work my side of the street only, and over here it felt like a small honoring of the more than 11 years of joy and wonder, grace and sharing everything we had. I'm glad I sent it.

I was sitting on a stone bench at the end of the high 'Bluff Trail' walk a while ago, I always sit there before heading back down, and I did some sobbing. I suppose I made myself cry by playing sad songs on my phone, and maybe that's a "Duh" to the ninth degree. But it felt, and feels, right. I'm sad. My old friend and mentor Dick M would say, like he always did when he was still around, "You're right where you're supposed to be."

We were married on a mountaintop in Virginia in 2010. That was a happy day. Today, down here by the ocean in southern California, I have no one to love. And no one to be loved by. Today, right here in Encinitas I mean, there sure are people I love all over the place, and people who love me those places too. Just no one right here, right now, right here today.

I do know I could tell myself to shut up and tell myself to count all my blessings, and honestly I don't know if I could count that high. Compose cheerier words to end the week here in this Blog. But, it's mostly not where I'm at today. This feels like a day it's just alright for me to hold hands with sadness.

And, by the way – I do believe in Santa Clause. I'm just not certain if it's my anniversary or not.

monday

My friend Craig reminds me:

"Chop wood, carry water."

Jack Kornfield puts it this way:

"First the enlightenment, then the laundry."

Directions on the box.

the only one

I was in the Pacific Ocean last Saturday afternoon, with my boogie board. It was cloudy and gray, not so many people. Some guy was maybe 10 yards away from me and my lane of more unsuccessful rides than successes – each day a new day. He kept looking at me and at one point yelled over some advice, I believe, as to how I could do better. I did not hear what he said, but I yelled back thanks.

About 15 minutes later, after one of my faster, longer, bitchin' rides, and when it was obvious he was getting ready to leave the water, he came over through the water to me and asked me how old I was. I said 72, and when I did his face lit up and he got this great smile. He said something else, like that's great or cool or words like those. I was glad my birth certificate could be the source of a bit more happiness on the planet. Even, maybe, hope for that guy's (someday) older age.

I was in the Pacific again early this morning – Tuesday morning – before nine, my first time out for a morning boogie. It was again gray and clouded over and the water temperature had dropped a few degrees. But I went out into the sea. Way over to my right was a lone surfer on his board and way over to my left was another lone surfer. As for me, I was the only person in the water at Moonlight Beach. The only one in the water.

I wondered if maybe I was the only boogie boarder in the Pacific Ocean at that very moment. Such a glittery thought.

My life, these days, is chock full with stuff. Good times,

hard times; joys and sorrows; moments of wonder, like this morning, and moments of tears. Suit up and show up they told me, a long time ago, and that's what I've been trying to do the best I can each day of this last half year. And now I honestly don't know how long I'll get to have this ocean by my side – within my easy reach. My future's up in the air.

Why suiting up (bathing suiting) and showing up this morning, even for only about seven or 10 minutes, was exactly the right thing for me today, a couple of hours before heading off to offer a few more laughs to the San Marcos kids. The joy is in the journey, right?

And, as Pema Chodron says – "This is all the path we have."

upside Down

I had two guys leave me messages that they may know a place for me to move to, as the word's getting around, and it turns out they both had the same place in mind. And it turns out I thanked them unendingly for thinking of me, because it's wicked lonely out here on the edge of the continent being the new kid, and I implied I was going to think about it and lean toward saying 'No', which in my case, with my notice and last day here in my current room rushing toward me, and sleeping in my car just a bit more possible, you'd think I'd be falling on my knees and running toward the referred oasis.

Who knows? Maybe I will, a week from today, or a week from Saturday, if there remain no leads on where I can land my withered but still cute little butt next. The description of their referred place just felt like my 'No' was more of a 'Yes' in this world of mine today, on this path of mine today, the path – Pema says – is the only one I've got.

So, I'll keep signing up on roommate sites and I'll keep answering Craigslist posts and if I answer 100 maybe I'll hear from two – I have a hunch it's a straight, old guy thing – and like my long-ago high school friend Donnie would say, "All you can do is all you can do." And even my tentative 'No' feels within the realm of those don't-drink-a-day-at-a-time folks' language of "going any lengths" and "asking for help with complete abandon" and my own forever goal of being "all-in" in whatever it is I'm doing.

I came back a minute ago from Moonlight Beach and another foray into the big ocean with my boogie board. My ass was thoroughly kicked on the biggest wave I misjudged, big ouch, and I missed some others with poor timing and I caught some because little by slow I'm "getting it". And sometimes there is a speed thing and a rushing over and through the water thing which is both scary and like a crazy good Halloween fright, has me yelling "yippee". Anyway, how blessed am I to be out in the ocean on a green-and-blue board under a sunny blue sky the tail end of September, knowing I'm staring the possible end of those days straight on.

Late afternoon ravings here, in Encinitas, on a glorious day in which my birth certificate has not changed a smidge and I remain well under the influence of all-in sobriety, and periodically I say, to myself, "Wow, what a great adventure." And hope for the sun to come up and out again tomorrow.

a come to meeting

I had what my old pal Judge Joe Will called a "Come to Jesus meeting" with myself this morning. It occurred during a 25 minute, 25 second timed-writing session, and as the clock wound down I got more crazed, more agitated, more electric in my admonition to myself to let it all hang out, Bud, you're lookin' at nowhere to go.

September's all but run out, the calendar whispered to me as I began writing, and the 30-day notice you gave – my mind chimed in – means three weeks and you're outta here. Means no address, Bro, nowhere to forward mail, nowhere to ship the bed, get all those books and paint supplies and paintings I've painted back in boxes and double Trader Joe's bags, begin to load the car again – of which, now, here in Encinitas time, some of that sacred storage space belongs to not one but two boogie boards. So, I wrote and wrote and it became a frenzy and the all-in's and the any lengths and the complete abandon's jumped off the screen, right smack into my mind's eye. It's October tomorrow, kid, and I've promised myself a Keto-busting pizza on Halloween (idea coming from overheard San Marcos kid convo), and.......

it does not matter if it's hard, or feels like rotten luck, or if there's a whisper it's all too much, twice in half a year, the big "Now where do I go?" That don't matter. Glue your butt to the computer seat, Holmes, staple your fingers to this keyboard, Brah, and send out 10,000 requests and replies and responses and even a bit of begging's all-over greater San Diego to find a place to live. Today. Do it today.

Judge Joe Will would have looked on all this, these last few hours here for me in Encinitas, and shook his head in approval. "Yup, that right there, that's a fo' sure Coming to Jesus meeting."

He'd of been right.

why not

Here's me, oh crazy Friday, wishing you (my reader) – and me – the happiest and most joyous of weekends.

Maybe with a little cool magic thrown in as well.

Cause, why not?

a little this, some of that

Yesterday afternoon, Sunday, I was driving in search of a motel with a proposal for long-term stay at reduced rate (didn't happen) when the Kate Bush song "Running Up That Hill" came on 91X, my favorite San Diego radio station which comes in clearly about 75% of the time and is actually broadcast from Tijuana. Her song – long ago I owned the LP where it can be found – felt exactly appropriate for me, yesterday, here now in Encinitas, here in October. Running up that hill. I'm in need of a new place to live, a safer and healthier space in which to land, and my Craigslist account is broken and won't let me make posts for needing a room in the communities I'd like to find one; the internet here in this room works on a whimsical basis, maybe 50% of the time – way less than 91X clarity; there are really no people here with whom I'm close, not really, who are looking out for me the way so many of you and so many others have and did right after the divorce and its fall-out time back there in mid-April. Running up a hill.

Saturday I drove to Ocean Beach, a spiritual place for me many years now, to look for a place to live – posting up my need on a 'meeting' bulletin board; walking up and down streets looking for "room for rent" signs in windows; stopping strangers on the street and asking if they knew of any. I also managed to get into the water with my boogie board and for the first time ever away from the main beach by the pier, all the way over to Dog Beach. There, much to my amazement and it turns out joy, I discovered this nearly never-ending sandbar straight out from the shore, and it caused big waves breaking far out beyond my poor-swimming comfort level to gather up water and re-form in closer. I had my best day yet boarding, and I was able to look from side to side on my rides and see that I was traveling nearly at the speed of light, like my seven and eight and nine-year old boogie peers – my now sacred, giggling cadre. Amidst all the unknowns and fears these days, it was pure bliss. Oh, Keto-busting delight at Hodad's too.

I've been feeling like only one person in my life truly "gets it", the "it" being clear about my life situation today, even though I've been talking about it here in the Blog and out there in the world for weeks now. That's my long-time pal and best friend and old boss and ongoing mentor Gavin in Oakland. Lately I've had long telephone talks with Kate and Joyce up there in greater Portland, Oregon, and they've listened and they get it too. The "it" being the "groundlessness" in my life right here today, early this Monday morning. So, I'll share the facts one more time, and not with any "poor me" or "why me" or any of that. I'm on my path, the one the Great Spirit wants me on, and I'm unendingly grateful to still be here to be on it, and so interested for what comes next. And, yes, just a little scared.

My move-out date is October 22, a Friday. Gotta be out by then. I will begin packing my things here in my room October 9, next Saturday. I'm going to begin, in earnest and with absolutely no shame, October 13, a Wednesday, asking people I've come to know a little down here if I can crash on their couch a while. Because I have nowhere to go. My plan is to actually be moved out of here by Sunday the 17th, waking up close enough the next day where I can get to my amazingly wonderful "job" working with the San Marcos kids the 18th and 19th.

After that, I haven't got a clue.

Also, I predict this week's posts here at "Couch Surfing" will be short and sweet. It's a time thing. And, my long-time readers, the plan is for these Monday-through-Friday daily posts to come to an end the 22nd of this month. That has long been my plan, I'll explain why another day. Now it's somewhat ironically become the "notice" day for me as well.

Those don't-drink-one-day-at-a-time folks have a line in one of their books which says this – "We stood at the turning point."

Yup.

something borrowed

Tuesday borrowing a Sunday haiku….

Life here, on the down low, exquisitely sparse

wax on

Oh, we had the most incredible lightning and thunder storm here in southern California Monday night. Lightening dancing and slashing and raging across the sky. Mother Nature's electric psychedelics – all her way. Many thousands in San Diego were left without power. We were fortunate here in Encinitas – power remained.

I had swept the long driveway with the heavy push broom earlier before heading off for a sweet day of tenderness with the San Marcos kids, what some may mistakenly call 'work'. By Tuesday morning, the previous night's storm having departed and left behind an absolutely pristine, balmy day, the driveway was covered more than ever with Torey Pine needles and cones. I went back out there a couple hours ago, in lieu of my everyday (except this one) morning walk, because I wanted things to look neat and nice when the home owner returns today from an across-the-Atlantic trip. And also, because I wanted the mesmerizing monotony of push here, push here, push here, now there. Attention all-in, leave no needle behind. Call it wax on, wax off. You know what I mean.

If my life, from this moment forward here early Wednesday, continues as it has a while now – screwy, amazing, scary, entirely wide-open for most anything – maybe tomorrow (as I picked up an extra shift with the kids today), maybe tomorrow when I make my way over to the Pannikin coffee shop and I'm at a small second-level outdoor table reading or writing or daydreaming or just there in hopes of inspiration, maybe someone will ask if they can share the table and I'll say, "Sure", without looking up. Then I will look up, and sitting down to hang out with me for just a little while will be Mr. Miyagi. I bet you know him. Smiling softly, sternly too. "You know what to do," he'll say, expression unchanged. "Wax on, wax off. Wax on, wax off."

And I won't then, and I don't now, need to hear anything else. Chop wood and carry water, kid. Wax on, wax off,

Brah. Just do the next indicated thing. Be bold. Have some courage. Have some faith.

Cause, what else is there, kid?

Thurs

No internet. Nuttin' much new. Suit up, show up they said. What I got.

Gods there be

No internet left in rented room, no log-in capability with library network. Recently read in a book about surfing – one guy's life philosophy is the gods are toying with us. There are likely reasons for all this. Don't ask me, I'm working on where to sleep at night.
While here in the Encinitas library, the Pacific over there out the windows, here on my phone, my understanding quotient pretty darn low.
Even for a Friday.

groovin' for Monday

on a Sunday afternoon, Starbucks patio, they closed early, not enough staff. Internet completely broken in rented room, cannot post on the laptop here, won't let me, on phone now with early extra San Marcos kids shift tomorrow, time racing toward Encinitas ending, there may be a chance or two for a new home this week, boogie boarding an hour ago, the kid so-so at best.

I want to say everything is broken. Like Dylan sings it. But it ain't. These are just these times.

And every so often, from the corner of my eye, I see the mischievous cat. Goofy grin and all.

well, well, well

Here I am Monday morning writing Tuesday's possible post, I wonder what the day-ahead-of-time composing this week means? Or maybe it doesn't mean anything other than stuff in my life doesn't work and then other stuff does and my best bet is to be alert for the openings and grateful if and when they come. And pounce.

So, I'm here early with the San Marcos kids covering someone else's shift plus my own, and there's a birthday in the house which is cool beans and celebrations, balloons and the kind of plain old joys we all need – all of us and the whole-wide world. And what I want to say now this morning – and it'll be just as cool and encouraging posted tomorrow – is to report a distinct and clear sense I had a while back there in the Encinitas room earlier today of being okay. Being alright. Cared for and looked after. I felt it and I knew it, and any worries and cousins of angsts hovering about these last few days and weeks were gone in that moment. Floated up and fizzled away. This is gratitude as I experience it.

I'll be living somewhere else soon enough and it'll be cool and I'll be alright, how could it be any other way with the friends I have and the grinning Universe and, duh, two boogie boards. Such an amazingly generous world, my sliver of it. Hiccups and all.

late Wednesday

when you read this I will be getting ready for, on my way to, in the middle of, or having completed a get-together with a guy down in San Diego proper who responded to the one Craigslist post I was able to slip through the censors, and who said he wanted to talk with me about the potential roommate thing. Sitting here typing this now, I don't know what will happen.

I can, though, tell you what I hope happens – or has happened by the time you're reading. I hope he likes me and I like him and his doggy likes me (i.e., not viewed as a fun chew toy), and I hope the space feels like enough for me, the small he described on the phone being relative, and with enough room for my bed and maybe a couple other things, and somewhere to type, which could be in his already lived-in space if that's cool, or even the Starbuck's right next door – 15 feet doorway to doorway. What I hope the most is it feels right – like, "yeah, this should happen" right – and we shake hands and I write him a check and I leave from above downtown San Diego later tonight, an October 13th, with a new place to live. A new address. A new life experience directly waiting down the path. Some comfort.

If it goes the way I hope it goes I'll be farther from the sacred Pacific Ocean than here in Encinitas, but not much farther, and actually a sideways, fun-way to get there through the downtown city and up and over a really big peninsula hill and rolling directly down to Ocean Beach, which I love – with its great sandbar for boogie boarding, its extra special pier for ocean, surfer, and sunset viewing, its wicked funky multi-colored vibe, and a pretty cool eating establishment called Hodad's – that I may have mentioned once or twice here on the 'Couch' before.

Then, here in the Blog Thursday, assuming I find an internet signal through which to work, I'll let you know. Either I'll have a new place to live and in which to rejoice still being above ground and at which to continue with expanding my generous life – dig it, sharing the me of me. Or I won't, and I'll mostly be back to dangling on the breeze. And yes, there are for sure worse places to be than on the breeze. And also, yeah – I'm a little weary of the dangling.

25 miles down the road

I found a new place to live late yesterday afternoon. In San Diego. Pretty much where I'd dreamed of living from shortly after the day my former wife Susan told me she wanted a divorce – which was exactly six months ago today. Back there then in her Portland living room, the thought came to me – you can go to San Diego. I aimed to make it happen with all I had to give, and found myself 10 weeks later 25 miles from my target, and back in the ocean. But that turned out to be simply a way station along the way – a stop-off place of gods with boogie boards, gliding pelicans and moonlight palms, and other watery things –

Now, three and a half months later, I have shaken hands with a young guy, he's welcomed me into his long-time home – the home of him and his pooch – and by this time next week I'll be moved in, such as that is. In need of minimal furniture, a physically healthier self than I woke to this morning, and a big pocketful of ongoing and expanding wonders and daydreams and outs of this world –

Still a kid – still thrilled, and blessed, to get to take it all in.

Oh, San Diego.

keeping on

I'm out here on the patio early, there's no internet signal in the room I rent. The room I have rented and paid for through next Friday, the 22nd, which is also the date I have long considered as the end to these somewhat infamous Monday through Friday postings. Maybe it'll go that way, maybe it won't. Here on the laptop, always a somewhat freaky and less than comfortable device for a desktop kid like me, I'm as far into the planning stages of my life as the next hour. That's about it. In fact, I came out here simply to see if there was a signal to be had, yet when I discovered one, opened the Blog and ran right here to 'Couch Surfing at 70' to get something down and done for the day.

The longer plan I do have, with slightly more expansive thinking, is continue picking up and cleaning up and packing up the rented room – which is being shown to the next perspective tenant around me today. The packing and moving thing is a lot, second time in six months, and the fact I don't feel well feels understandable. I'm weary. I'm not down. I'm not empty of excitement for what may be waiting just around the corner. I'm not not thrilled I woke up again today, cause I am. I'm still here and I'm thinking I have some crazy big plans for when I find myself 25 miles in the direction of Mexico, hopefully permanently next Wednesday or Thursday. No – I remain filled with delight and wonder and the sense of ongoing, ever-present grace. Just a little tired is all.

My hope for today is keep getting "it" together, head over to Moonlight for righteous boogie boarding early afternoon when the weather folks are promising 80 degrees – maybe the last hot day of the year. Then come back and do a few more things and head back down to the beach for the Friday night dinner I've had every single week I've been here in Encinitas – a veggie burrito at Filiberto's. Then over to a Moonlight bench with a bag of cashews and a stroll over to D Street, and I promise I'll be completely alive rejoicing I was allowed to discover and twirl and rejoice in these places. Then back to the rented room and sleep, and if I'm lucky to wake up again tomorrow, another boogie time in the spot of ocean in which I've learned to do it, followed by a mid-afternoon cruise down the 5 to SD and Golden Hill and the first of two actual movings of my things. Ima be a Golden Hill kiddo.

It's good to have goals, I always say, and I have a few the next 48 hours or so. They all seem to fall very nicely within the ever-fun and delightful milieu of keeping on keeping on.

it's just a jump to the left

Oh, dizzy Monday morning, you begin for me in a small room just off the sidewalk along B Street in the Golden Hill neighborhood of San Diego. Sweet San Diego. Me, channeling my best Stevie Wonder – "Just like I pictured it." I sit on the edge of the bed on the floor, and I couldn't guess, never mind imagine, who's slept in it before, but I sit on it this morning in silence, in the dark save for the street light glowing through the slatted blinds, for 22 minutes, either something akin to meditation or else an experience exactly like it. I don't believe there's a difference, long as I'm aware there's something goin on. I put on sweatshirt and jacket against the chill, slip out the door at 5:15, a genuine cheery goodbye to the pit bull on the floor, stow the last stuff in my car and drive out of the gated-lot and over and around to B Street and a space in which to pull over and hop out and get a large Starbuck's for the road and the high-speed drive back here to Encinitas.

Much of the stuff I own in the world that isn't back in Joyce's garage in Portland has been left in Golden Hill where I will begin to live all the moments of my days ahead beginning Wednesday. Coupla days here to wrap this Encinitas gig up, have the easier drive to show up and be of some service to the San Marcos kids today and tomorrow. Then the boogie-board kid points the Camry south on the 5 Wednesday in the a.m. and thereafter does his Pacific glides and slides and light-speed rides next to Dog Beach in OB on into the future.

Did I live in Golden Hill in some other life? A different physical existence, reveling and celebrating in the ain't no thing like me but me reality of it all? Doing the time warp – again and again and again?

And will I ever be the same?

note to self

pay wicked good attention….. be really generous sharing me with folks out there in the world – especially the San Marcos kids today….. find a storage facility and rent a space and get my stuff out of Joyce's garage back there in Portland cause she deserves her space back and she's been such a true friend, loyal and always there, and what's greater than that….. make a deal with a moving company which I hope they don't turn out to be wacky and/or crooked….. come on – have some faith, Brah….. drop in Friday morning to the San Diego senior center out of which a woman named Maria has been supporting me since I very first figured that heading all the way down there to SD was my path….. forget my thought-about October 22 ending of this daily Blog and go on writing and posting and blogging forever….. consider boogie boarding at OB Thursday afternoon even if the water's getting too cold and the overall planet temp ain't quite as hot as they think it might be, so's to better warm my ancient but still-cute butt….. keep paying wicked good attention….. keep shining….. please finish my un-finished books, will ya!!….. make Golden Hill the center of my world, includes great coffee shops and beauteous walks….. start painting again, Bro, like pdq….. nourish this grateful heart of mine, kind of like the Isley Brothers' heart, except this one's mine….. go tell it on the mountain…..

more

Beep beep.

dateline OB

Let's see, quick here, left just after noon from here up on the hill and rolled down Broadway to the harbor, you cling along the edge by all numbers of ultra-fancy yachts and other nautical means of transport and fun, directly past the airport on your right, then a jigsaw directional to the top of

Point Loma and another point down, this one crazy steep, wait, see straight out there, the biggest of big blue waters and the famed Ocean Beach pier and I know the way and hang a right and a left and park on Brighton and hoof it with boogie board under arm, me and the board buffeted by fairly wicked winds.

Then I arrive at the beach – they plowed up a berm since I was last there and dragged all the life-guard stations into a little no-one's-home community – and the only kids in the water have wet suits and surf boards and I'm happy and maybe the teensiest of proud to say your blogging story-teller dragged off running shoes and tank top and hat and walked right out there into the Pacific. It was not the level of frigid I worried over – not much worry, to keep it real, I think I've gone around a corner on all that and landed squarely in "just be here now", but to keep these facts accurate the sand bar bottom had shifted and my feet kept dropping into holes which kind of weirded me out, never self-described as much of a swimmer, so I hung back and took a number of 'weak-ass' rides and after maybe 17 minutes decided to cool it, and this journalistic exercise in filling this space happily reports my final ride was the best, long and quick and me yahoo-ing.

Then I walked back to the Camry, stowed the board in the trunk and the towel over the driver's seat and took a long bathing-suit drying walk into what you could call the 'downtown' of OB and out on the pier and walked by Hodad's without going in, mostly to show me I could do it, got primarily naked back in the car – bathing suit off, cargo shorts on – and did all that driving stuff nearly in reverse with the exception of a detour to a Trader Joe's my ex-Susan and I had discovered on one of our five-night OB stays, and I shopped and drove on back and strolled into my small and ever-so-sweet little room and hit the space bar and the screen asked, "You forgetting something?" And I like to answer "Nah" whenever I get the chance,

So, nah.

it's nine months

Today, October 22, is the day I long thought I would end these Monday through Friday daily posts, I can't say it's so much a lack of subject matter and fear of repeating myself, which I do sometimes and I know I've learned much in my life only through repetition so I ain't gonna apologize if I say "the me of me" 20 times, it even helps me rejoice in the self-awareness, no the reason for the "end it here" thinking is that it was back exactly nine months ago, January 22, also a Friday, when I posted in Couch Surfing I was going to begin posting every day, Monday through Friday, going forward, and that these posts would consider and report on what I called my "daily weather", so call it the internal milieu of me – make that moi – and sometimes the words would run on something like endlessly and sometimes there could be a single word – how I am that day – and I'm glad to say I have not missed one weekday since that long-ago Friday in the dead of winter, when I was back there in Portland and I thought happily married and living with the kids, Susan's and mine, and doing the things we'd made our own, one of which was this Blog for me, Couch Surfing at 70 which I'd got going sometime back in 2018.

This particular Friday (Jan 22) I was spelling out what felt like personal frustration with myself for inconsistency as a blogger, like maybe I'd write three days in a row and then my life would step forward past the Blog thing and two weeks would pass without a single post, and I can't speak for anyone else but that didn't feel right to me, it felt cheaping out on a responsibility I'd taken on when I promised to be blogging, like, regularly. So, as I do every once in a while, I had a come to Jesus meeting with myself and said I'm gonna commit to write and post five times a week and since I don't want to run out of material and since from the get-go back in '18 this Blog was commited to leave politics and other everyday social considerations outside the door, what better than write about how I "was" that day.

So that's the history and I haven't missed a day, I said, I think there may have been two days with just photos but it still represented, and somewhere along the way Marie in Scotland – my original Patron – said she loved this stuff – which got rather heavy and more urgent and maybe more cutting edge when the divorce came into my life in mid-April. Anyway Marie said she loved it and it would make for a great book, and whether she put that thought in my head or if I'd been thinking about it my own self earlier, pretty much right from then that's what I decided to do- and here encouraging you to let go any potential feelers of guilt when you already know there's no way you'll be buying that book, it's cool, like Dr. Frankenfurter told Janet Wise in "Rocky Horror" when she sort of dissed his creation, "I didn't make him for you." So, it's cool, we'll remain friends, and par for the course is losing money on nearly every self-published book and I don't even care, it's kind of a "legacy" thing, maybe my kids will think about me and think about my books when I'm gone, or not – but the planet knows.

So, blah de blah, I began collecting all my daily posts from January 22 on and have most of them gathered in what will become a book until a couple of weeks ago when I found myself moving – again!! – yup, for the second time in six months and I am freakin' weary, kids, and the fact is my desktop computer which holds all my posts and the tentative paperback – spoiler alert, to be titled "Weather" – that computer is in pieces in a box on the floor over there cause I've got no desk, or chair on which to sit at a desk I don't have, and I'm two days into a brand new life – it's not a new chapter, it's a brand new life and nothing could be more clear – to me- so there's a delay and who knows how long it'll go on and I'm not sweating it, things have a way of working, I mean, here I am typing in a small but way fun room in Golden Hill in San Diego and if you'd of told me that five years ago I would have been dumbfounded and telling it to me this morning veers heavily into some mystical place – which will be its own post here maybe next week – To get back to the point, somewhere along the way I decided my "Weather" book would be just swell with exactly nine months, which is today, and so I offered the thought it would be all over but the hoopla today.

Then life happened and I landed here, rejoicing all the way, and I said both to myself and to a sunny afternoon, Nah, I've got new stuff promising to show up and worth saying, so these posts will go on and you can look for one Monday, but in fact the book ends today, with the final period coming real soon now, and I'll sell it cheap and if you are at least somewhat hip you'll probably pick up a copy.

I would.

Afterword

I've just finished – not even a minute ago – reading nine months of weekday Blog posts which I'd lifted, copied, and pasted from Couch Surfing at 70. Some were boring. There was much repetition, repeated as different takes on the same emotions and habits, awareness's and choices. I said somewhere along the way – was it back in the Intro? – I consider repetition a good thing. Lord knows most of what I've learned which matters in this world is as a result of hearing it or seeing it or being subjected to it over and over and over. It's a good thing

Everything was not repetitive, though, and much was not boring. Not to these eyes. How could a human life reported on with sharpened-by-circumstance honesty be such a thing as boring. It may not be everyone's cup of tea – and there'll be no offense taken. But, cross my heart – pinky swear – it's all real.

I was taken back by some of these daily truth-telling reports. Some were damn fine. Quality writing. Reminding me, yeah, I am a writer. Been one in some shape or form most my life. I believe there's proof of that statement here. There were also times I burst into tears. Quite a few. Maybe it was the excellence of reporting emotion. More likely it was because memories – many of them difficult – were energized and materialized back to the front of my mind. My heart too. Remembering that day – oh, yeah. I guess it's to be expected. I showed up at the keyboard and said this is how I am today. Honest.

There's also, for me, a remarkableness to it all too. Genuine "Wows". Really real "Holy Cows". A few "Oh my Gods".

That's what happened when I read from this day, then from that day.

If you are here, you've hung in and are now reading this Afterword, I thank you. You know me better. I started way up there and I ended way down here. Nine months of a 72-year-old's life. Portland, Oregon to San Diego, California. Joyously married, alone in a long-dreamed of place. Retired, now back at work. Oh, can you say boogie board?

Nearly all of it would have been beyond any imagination I could have possibly summoned, back there the third week in January of this year. If, say, someone had pulled me aside, whispered, "Hey, you know what?"

But it all did.

And that's that. The Monday through Friday Blog posts go on. My life goes on, I'm very happy to say.

I go on.

And so do you.

Made in the USA
Columbia, SC
24 November 2021